REAR-VIEW REFLECTIONS *on* RADICAL CHANGE

A Green Grandma's Memoir and Call for Climate Action

LINDA MARY WAGNER

Also by Linda Mary Wagner
Unearthing the Ghosts: A Mystery Memoir
Available in paperback from TBMBooks.com and Amazon
Available in eBook from Amazon

Rear-view Reflections on Radical Change:
A Green Grandma's Memoir and Call for Climate Action

ISBN(Print Edition): 979-8-35094-321-4
ISBN (eBook Edition): 979-8-35094-322-1

Published by Buried Gems LLC, Linda M. Wagner, Founder.

Cover Design, Printing, e-Book, and distribution by bookbaby.com.

Copy Editor & Proofreader: Sue Toth.

Encouragement & segment critiques from: Women at Woodstock Virtual Writer's Colony, The Write Practice, and the Nonfiction Authors Association.

Website design of https://lindamarywagner.com by Karen VanGorp.

Marketing support from Caitlin Du Bois, Of the Wood LLC and Katie McAnally, Rooted Yarrow.

Lifetime support, as always, from my spouse Barry, children Nathan & Joanna, & my wonderful siblings: Joan, Carol, Diane, Richard, and Betty.

Dedicated to my children and their spouses and children.

Age narrows fields
of vision
but unfolds
some richer quilt
a multicolored patchwork

From "A Room of Our Own"
Linda M. Wagner
Spring 1978

TABLE OF CONTENTS

DECADE V Plus: 2010 – 2022
Back to the Future: Age 58-70

PROLOGUE:

Revolution

To utter the word "revolution" is to stir feeling.

Sometimes that is the only purpose. As an 18-year-old in 1970, I intended the Revolution to stir feelings for Vietnamese children, Black Americans, and girls around the world. I thought that compassion alone could end the war, provide equal opportunity, and free half the human race. I thought it could end a beige and gray culture and usher in rainbows of color to fashion, music, and art.

By the time I was 21 and a college student in the city of Buffalo, where the skies had turned red from pollution and the men were turned away from the closing steel and auto factories, I intended the Revolution to stir not only feelings but action. The Revolution would lead people to march in the streets to end all wars, legalize pot, protect the environment, and make a classless society with jobs for everyone. The interlocking corporate directorates would become transparent, and their power would yield to the workers. The mentally ill would be freed from cruel state hospitals into loving communities of halfway homes. In a short time, the engines of war would turn to life supporting ventures and the promise of government of, by, and for The People would be realized.

The People did march, and the war in Vietnam did end. Psychedelic colors and sounds entered the mainstream. Capitalism allowed cooperatives for wholesome food to flourish. New countercultural business ventures began. News media reported where the true powers in society reside. And some Black Americans were granted opportunities that had been denied them in the past. The increased availability of birth control and the Roe v. Wade decision changed the calculus for girls and women who considered their futures, leading many to choose careers that their mothers and grandmothers had never imagined for themselves.

On the other hand, pot was not legalized, and many young Black men ended up with long prison sentences. Meanwhile, most young white men and women got off easy if they got caught. The strength of labor unions that had once delivered handsome wages and benefits to American working men, most white and even some Black, withered into ghostly memories. Entrepreneurial ventures that appeared revolutionary in 1975 calcified into corporate power centers. Cultural rainbows of soft color and acoustic sound turned into cold steel and heavy metal. Wages at the bottom froze. Wealth at the top blossomed. The homeless population grew. The weapons industry flourished at home and abroad. Analog became digital. Phones were freed from their static receivers for full mobility, while minds became imprisoned by them.

Five decades have passed. On May 25, 2020, a Black man in Minneapolis named George Floyd died after a police officer named Derek Chauvin kneeled on his neck for nine minutes and 23 seconds. Advocates from the Black Lives Matter movement have made a revolutionary call to "Defund the Police."

On January 6, 2021, a mob of Trump-loving "Christian patriots," many of whom espouse white supremacy, overran the halls of the U.S. Congress, killing one police officer and savaging dozens more, while hunting to hang elected officials who dared to defy their leader. They said that they are The Revolution now and they have stirred far more than feeling. Their reality was a horror show for most Americans who witnessed it on television or online. They were guided by "alternative facts" spun by an anonymous character known only as "Q," promoted by a fascist authoritarian who was elected by a minority of eligible USA voters in 2016 and amplified by a variety of traditional and social media platforms, including Fox News, Newsmax, Twitter, Facebook, and others in the deep recesses of online twisted minds.

If "Q & A" still means Question and Answer, what does The Revolution mean to me now? If the Q was the Question, Who or What is the A for Answer?

POTUS #46 was elected, certified, and inaugurated. That may be one part of the Answer. But even though Joe Biden is a great guy, I would hardly consider him The Revolution. Even Bernie Sanders, an avowed Democratic Socialist and enormously popular social media meme with his Inaugural Day mittens in January 2021, is not The Revolution.

The Revolution is not a particular person at all. It is the ever-changing activity of making our voices heard and taking political steps to ensure that those voices acquire the power needed for fundamental change toward a better world. But when you don't make clear what you need and want once you have that power, your Revolution is bound to fade and die, or be co-opted by devious, shadowy, corrupt forces who are driven purely by narcissistic control and unfettered greed.

I would prefer not to think about "Revolution" now. I would rather live out my remaining years enjoying grandchildren, traveling, taking interesting courses, living in peace and prosperity with all my neighbors, drawing, observing flowers, birds, and waterfalls, and writing verse about natural wonders. But I can do none of those things for very long if I do not use my voice to gain power on behalf of those natural wonders, especially on behalf of my children and grandchildren.

Revolution is often contrasted with Evolution, not the Darwinian evolution of living creatures, but the social and political evolution of human society. After 70-plus years on the planet Earth, more than 50 of which have included some conscious observation of the social and political world around me, I have concluded that Revolutions are not one-time cataclysmic events, but that they evolve over the span of one or more generations.

Hence, I offer this collection of writings to share my 50-plus-year evolution of a 1972 American Yippie, who considered it a revolutionary act when I stole a copy of Abbie Hoffman's 1970 *Steal this Book*. The collection here follows up on stories told about the years 1952 to 1973 in my 2013 book, **Unearthing the Ghosts: A Mystery Memoir**.

It is my hope that this collection of writings can move people toward the ultimate goal of my personal revolution – Common Ground for Mutual Good, regardless of who or where you are. Further, it is my most profound belief, based on a consensus formed through decades of scientific research and analysis, that the revolution and evolution most urgently needed today is centered on mitigating and reducing climate change to ensure the future survival of all forms of life on planet Earth.

DECADE I: 1970 - 1979

Young Adulthood: Age 18 - 27

Radicalization's Origins and A Feminist Wave

On many car mirrors, it states, "Images in the mirror appear further away than they are." This is also true when considering the impact of past traumas upon a person's psychological well-being.

A tsunami of revolutionary trends overwhelmed American social and political life between my middle school and senior years in high school. They immersed me like floodwaters in challenges to my conservative Catholic childhood. Between 1963 and 1970, my personal life and that of all teenagers was backdropped by moving images of assassinations, brutal assaults against Black American civil rights activists, horrific scenes from the Vietnam War, and ominous warnings about environmental disasters – all broadcast live into our living rooms on daily TV newscasts.

I was a serious, pensive child who read newspapers and watched news and public affairs programming with nearly as much religious fervor as I had displayed towards the Stations of the Cross. With only occasional comic relief embedded in my persona, the tragic events that surrounded the 1960s initiated a radicalization in me that was further cemented by a coming-of-age trauma. Detailed in my 2013 memoir, *Unearthing the Ghosts: A Mystery Memoir*, the story is summarized in the first essay in this section titled "The Research Psychiatrist's Subject."

The essay and memoir describe the extremely questionable treatment that Dr. Anthony A. Sainz delivered to me when I was 17. While doing research to reveal who Dr. Anthony A. Sainz really was, I discovered the following brief bio from Psychiatric Quarterly, January 1957:

> *Anthony Sainz, M.D. Dr. Sainz is head of the pharmacological research unit at Marcy (N.Y.) State Hospital. He has been active in the work of developing and evaluating phenotropic (sic) drugs for the last six years and is the author of scientific papers on this and other subjects. Born in Havana in 1915, he was graduated from the University of Havana Medical School in 1941. In Cuba, he did research for the Ministry of Public Health, for the Finlay Institute for Research of Havana, and the University of Havana Medical School.*

That background may seem impressive. Sainz did medical research during the first regime of Cuban dictator Fulgencio Batista, from 1941-44. However, my research also uncovered that in the U.S., this Dr. Anthony A. Sainz had advocated lobotomy for the mentally ill while practicing in Iowa during the 1950s, and that he had done extensive pharmaceutical experimentation on patients without their consent, using LSD, a variety of sedatives, and new "anti-psychotic" drugs pushed by the pharmaceutical industry.

Around 1972, Sainz disappeared from New York State after a court case in Iowa determined that he had committed a medically unethical offense against a man named Ernest Triplette. Sainz had given Triplette a drug "cocktail" of sedatives and LSD, and while the man was heavily medicated, the doctor led him to confess to the murder of a child. Because this maltreatment was hidden during Triplette's trial, Triplette was convicted and served 17 years in state prison. Subsequent evidence suggested that someone else had committed the child murder; furthermore, it was likely that the real murderer had killed at least one other child.

Triplette was released in 1972, after his pro bono attorneys gained access to his psychiatric medical records and successfully sued, as detailed in the book *Benefit of Law: The Murder Case of Ernest Triplette.* The central role that Sainz played in ordering the drugs given to Triplette is covered in pages 99-105 of that book. During the 17 years Triplette spent in prison, Sainz was allowed to continue his questionable pharmaceutical experiments on hundreds of patients with impunity.

In my case, I spent three weeks in early 1970 committed by Sainz, with my parents' permission, to the psychiatric ward of a Utica, New York Catholic hospital. I was 17 years old and in the middle of my senior year in high school. After my release from the hospital, I remained on a powerful anti-psychotic drug even though I was not psychotic. I was told to see Sainz weekly in his Rome, New York office, where he often attempted to hypnotize me.

Rome was the hometown of Griffiss Air Force Base, a major military installation during the Vietnam War and one of Rome, NY's largest employers when I lived there between 1964 and 1970. Many of my high school classmates were the children of military professionals. Our school encouraged debate about moral issues. During some of those debates, I expressed strong opposition to the war. I did not believe that the U.S. involvement in the Vietnam conflict met St. Augustine's "Just War" standard that was professed by the Catholic Church and my Catholic school. Some of my friends from military families agreed with me, but many did not.

Before encountering Dr. Sainz, I had begun exploring the philosophies of Western existentialists and mystics and religions of the Far East, such as Zen Buddhism and Hinduism. Since I was raised in the Roman Catholic Church, many among my family and friends, and the priests and nuns who taught me viewed concepts such as Ying/Yang and animism as heresy or apostasy. But these ideas expanded my world view, encouraging me to accept life on earth with all its contradictions, complexities, and cultures.

I turned 18 on my college campus in October 1970. By July 1, 1971, the 26th Amendment to the U.S. Constitution gave me the right to vote. So, the first time I was able to vote for U.S. President was November 1972, when I voted for the Democratic, anti-war candidate George McGovern and against the incumbent, Republican Richard Nixon. Despite growing opposition to the Vietnam War and the new youth vote, Nixon won in a landslide, and my candidate garnered less than 38% of the vote. This defeat and Nixon's later resignation under threat of impeachment solidified my view that more funda-mental action outside the electoral system was necessary to foster real change.

I had embraced the civil rights, integrationist movement led by Martin Luther King in the 1960s, and I sympathized with Black Americans who rioted after his assassination in 1968. I appreciated the voice of Malcolm X but, as a young white woman, I realized that the Black Power movement excluded me from direct participation in an ideology steeped in Black self-sufficiency. "Bury My Heart at Wounded Knee," first published in 1970, had opened my eyes and those of many others to the slaughter and betrayal of Native Americans throughout the history of white Western European exploration and settlement of the United States. It did not require a great intellectual leap to see connec-tions between the struggles of Blacks, indigenous peoples, and the Vietnamese against brutality, exploitation, and violence of a white supremacist ideology disguised as law and order, civilization, or democracy.

I could sympathize with the revolutionary fervor of marginalized groups. But the next rights movement was directly relevant to me. The feminist wave of the early to mid-1970s touched my core with the understanding, "The personal is political." In small, organized "consciousness-raising" groups on campus, open to women only, we shared personal stories about rape, incest, harassment, and other forms of abuse and discrimination. We learned documented women's history from mimeographed or photocopied pages and booklets about or by great women from the past. We discovered that we did not have equal rights to property, credit, or our own names. We discovered our own bodies and body parts that had been shielded under sheets by male gynecologists in an era when female doctors were nearly impossible to find.

At that time, "women's studies" programs were just emerging at colleges and universities. It is difficult to underestimate the explosive impact that these programs and organizing efforts had over time on public policy and our own personal lives as women. Launched most visibly by educated white women, the feminist movement also arose among Black and Latina women, both straight and lesbian. "R.E.S.P.E.C.T." sung by Black diva Aretha Franklin may have delivered a powerful message both to Black men and white America, but almost any woman felt that demand deep in her gut.

I took a course titled History of Science and Sexuality from a British professor named Elizabeth Fee in 1971 at the University at Binghamton, New York. A paper I wrote during that course responded to an essay written by the nineteenth century British journalist Walter Bagehot, who concluded, "We have, therefore, in fine, full ground for maintaining that the 'woman's-rights' movement' is an attempt to rear, by a process of 'unnatural selection,' a race of monstrosities—hostile alike to men, to normal women, to human society, and to the future development of our race." Bagehot's "science" stated that women's smaller brains signal their inferiority to men. I argued in my response that it is faulty logic to assume that smaller means inferior, because scientific evidence proves that smaller tools are often more efficient. I also challenged his illogical tautology that women who fight for equality are not "real" women.

Feminist networking and thought aided my personal recovery from the maltreatment by Dr. Sainz. Also essential in moving me forward was care from key friends, family, and a Jewish psychiatrist named Dr. Joseph Joel Friedman, who was Commissioner of Mental Health Services in Broome County, New York in the early 1970s. Dr. Friedman helped to free me from self-destructive feelings of guilt that originated with strict Catholic teaching and was cemented by my experience with Dr. Sainz. After meeting with Dr. Friedman weekly for several months in Binghamton, I felt self-confident and ready to move on with my life. I decided to transfer for a semester to the State University of New York campus in Buffalo in January 1973. It was there that, though mutual friends, I met a young male student named Barry from Long Island. Within weeks I fell deeply in love with him.

Nevertheless, on my spring break, I agreed to join my old friend Anne in an adventure, hitchhiking from Buffalo to Daytona Beach, Florida, an escapade that was both foolish and dangerous. We had good fortune on the first chunk of the trip, with kind drivers inviting us into their home for lunch and homemade pie or offering friendly advice and interesting conversation. But soon after reaching the deep South, our luck turned. First, two older men who picked us up tried to convince us to have sex, and when we said no, they pushed us out of the car at night on a lonely mountain highway. After we reached Florida, we made the mistake of getting into the back seat of a two-door car. Two young men drove off the highway to a remote corn field where the driver pulled out a gun and told us to do what they wanted. After raping us at gunpoint, they had the audacity to ask if we enjoyed it. I was certain we would wind up dead in that field. But they drove us back to the highway and let us out, saying, "Be careful of the cops. Hitchhiking is illegal in Florida."

Near the end of my first memoir, I told the full story of this encounter. When I returned to Buffalo, I told Barry what happened in a quiet, monotone voice, masking the terror I had experienced. His support, and having shared the whole experience with Anne, enabled me to move on from that trauma. Shortly after my return, I wrote the poem, Post Rape.

Around the same time that I moved from Binghamton to Buffalo, the U.S. Supreme Court issued one of its most momentous decisions.

From History.com

Roe v. Wade was a landmark legal decision issued on January 22, 1973, in which the U.S. Supreme Court struck down a Texas statute banning abortion, effectively legalizing the procedure across the United States. The court held that a woman's right to an abortion was implicit in the right to privacy protected by the Fourteenth Amendment to the Constitution.

During my last semester as a Philosophy major at the University at Buffalo, I took a course on ethics in which I was assigned readings from Plato, Aristotle, John Stuart Mills, Immanuel Kant, John Rawls, and Thomas Aquinas, and other philosophers. For our final written assignment, we had to address a contemporary moral issue, present opposing points of view, then reach and articulate our own conclusions.

There are few Supreme Court decisions that have had the revolutionary impact that the 1973 Roe v. Wade decision has had. In 1974, controversy over that relatively recent ruling appeared daily on the news and opinion pages of many newspapers. I reported on the controversies myself in the University at Buffalo student newspaper, The Spectrum. Hence, I chose to tackle that topic in my Ethics paper. With 13 years of Roman Catholic education under my belt, and the subsequent influence of feminist study and thought during my college days, I struggled to come to my own opinion.

I have never had to confront the question of whether to terminate my own pregnancy. I was a cautious and lucky utilizer of various forms of birth control until I decided I was ready to give birth. However, in 1974, two of my 21-year-old friends had recently had abortions, one with the consent of the man who impregnated her, and one without that consent. I heard the views of the individual women and men involved, and those discussions weighed heavily on me when I wrote the paper titled "Moral and Political Decisions on Abortion."

Nearly 50 years later, reading this undergraduate essay that I wrote in 1974, it is clearer than ever that Roe v. Wade was a revolutionary decision. However, the moral and political issues, feelings, and activism surrounding abortion have simmered and stewed ever since. The pendulum of political power over the lives of women swings hard indeed.

* * *

In the Fall of 1973, I moved into the off-campus apartment that Barry shared with his good friend Richie. After graduating with a B.A. in Philosophy and undeclared minor in Writing in June 1974, I worked for nearly a year in Buffalo while Barry finished his undergraduate studies and acquired big tips waiting on tables at an exclusive French restaurant. I also worked as a waitress, but at a fast-food, sit-down restaurant, and later as a clerk in the medical records department of the Roswell Park Cancer Research Hospital. In the records of patients at Roswell, I saw photos of horribly invasive cancer surgeries performed in the

1940s and '50s. It became clear that we should be grateful for a revolution in cancer treatment that has occurred and continues to advance 70 years later.

By the Spring of 1975, U.S. troops had finally withdrawn from Vietnam. A shamed Richard Nixon had resigned from the Presidency, under threat of impeachment over the Watergate burglary.

Barry and I had accumulated enough money to tackle a cross country road trip, made possible by my parents' college graduation gift of a Dodge Dart that we named "Big Blue" with much affection. We loaded camping and backpacking equipment in the trunk and took off to "look for America" (referencing Paul Simon's 1965 song, "America"). From Buffalo we drove to parts south, visiting Barry's parents who had recently moved to Florida, camping in Louisiana bogs during duck mating season, visiting my friend's mother in Biloxi, Mississippi where we caught shrimp and cooked them with tiny, boiled salt potatoes, packing gallons of water on our backs to climb over the very dry, desert side of the Guadalupe Mountains in Texas, driving up the west coast to San Francisco and beyond.

There were far too many adventures to remember and document here. But I did keep a journal, from which emerged poetry and prose included in this section.

By late August 1975, our travel funds had dwindled, and we tried to figure out together where to go and what to do next. Barry and I agreed that, amid a major recession, big cities were not the right place for us at that point in time. We ended up in Lexington, Kentucky, a smaller city that had jobs, since many opportunities had migrated from the North to the Southern part of the country. In addition, Barry's sister and her family were living there then. With my Roswell Park experience, I quickly landed a job as a hospital records clerk, alongside several middle-aged Black women and young Black and white men and women. Barry got work building houses, desiring to try a blue-collar life of physical labor. During evenings, I took typing lessons, to gain speed for the purpose of writing on a keyboard.

After a few months, I got a copywriting job at WLAP Radio, a commercial station that still produced some of its own commercials for local businesses. I was smitten with radio as a medium, but I was interested in journalism, not advertising. Eventually, Barry changed course, trading carpentry for a job at a law firm.

Given the economy, we were lucky to be employed. But we were suddenly facing life in a two-worker household at a purely personal level. After four years of college during which I had worked part-time at low-wage jobs, and four months of travel freedom with my "significant other," I was experiencing the basics of a full-time working life while trying to maintain a love relationship at home. We had smacked into reality's hard, brick wall, as you can tell from the pieces, When the Party Is Over, Hitting the Brick Wall, and the August 1975 journal entry that I wrote at that time.

When I was a child in the early 1950s, it was unusual for middle-class kids to have two working parents. The typical, white "Leave it to Beaver" family had a working dad and a stay-at-home mom who handled all the household chores. Those families may have been unaware of the Black American families whose mothers were out scrubbing floors, watching other women's children, and running small businesses in their own communities while they scraped to find someone to care for their own kids. Too many of those families were also missing a father who had to take work that kept them on the road, or working long hours at very low wages, or worse yet, ending up in prison for something they did or didn't do.

By the time I finished high school in 1970, the women's movement was making waves on the home front, with more women pushing their way into the work force at both high and low levels. Eventually, the economy figured out the benefits of allowing and enabling women – particularly white women – into the ranks of the paid employed. This was not always perceived as a good thing by men and women of color who found themselves competing for jobs with a flood of white women. But it also led to a stagnation in wages for all working people, whatever their gender or skin color.

This was never intended by women who took jobs outside the home. But the captains of industry, competing increasingly on a global stage, believed that the American middle class would tolerate lower wages for men if working women helped to increase household income, while they, the capitalists, profited from lower wages for everyone. I had become conscious of class advantages and disadvantages, but I did not understand the relationship between class, skin color, wealth, and caste until I read the book titled *Caste* by Isabel Wilkerson in 2021. The book clarified for me and many others how caste and racism reside within the institutions of societies worldwide, particularly those of the U.S.A.

In 1976, eager to move on from a year in the southern culture of Lexington, I applied to the Journalism graduate program at the University at Berkeley, California, while Barry applied to law schools. I was wait-listed at Berkeley, but my boyfriend got into a private law school near Berkeley and the public university in Buffalo. I sensed that he really wanted to return to the familiar world of New York State and attend the better of the two law schools, which was Buffalo. I feared that if I risked moving to Berkeley but not getting into school, we would both be miserable and likely to break up. With nearly a year of radio work under my belt, I became naively convinced that I could easily land a radio job in Buffalo. So, I followed my boyfriend to Buffalo. After making the move, I learned that I had been accepted, off the wait list, into Berkeley. By then, the idea of packing up again and risking a break-up with my boyfriend was more than I was willing to tackle.

I have often regretted that decision only because, in retrospect, I allowed fear to guide my actions, rather than my own passions and belief in myself. On the one hand, I am glad that I remained with a boyfriend whom I eventually married, with whom I have had children and grandchildren and many happy years. But on the other hand, I have come to recognize that anxiety has substantially limited my success in both personal and professional ways and that regret is too close to regression.

The Miscellaneous Buffalo Ruminations: 1976-1979, a Letter to the Editor of the Buffalo daily newspaper, and a group of Gender Parity poems from 1979 address some of these feelings of anxiety, regret, and emotional regression. I did not seek a therapist in those years, although it's likely I could have benefited from counseling. Some progress has been made in the treatment of mental illnesses such as generalized anxiety since the 1970s, but there remains the need for a true revolution for mental health. Few things have made this clearer than the impact that the SARS-COV2 pandemic has had on mental health since it began in 2020.

Getting back to the job market in Buffalo in the late 1970s, despite the feminist thought circulating on college campuses, post-graduate job searches and employment confronted me with sexual harassment more than once. As a waitress, one middle-aged male customer told me he'd like to take me "for a ride." On a job interview, the male radio jock with whom I met told me to go into the next room and take off my clothes because it was "time for the physical." Then he laughed and said he made it a point never to hire someone smarter than him. While working at a temporary job at a collections agency that promised computer training, but really had me stuffing envelopes, a man who visited deadbeat customers kicked the back of my chair repeatedly, saying, "I like to scare women." While working at a university-licensed public radio station, the head of the media studies department to whom the station manager reported asked me to lunch to discuss future opportunities, then made it clear that those opportunities were contingent on sexual favors. I declined.

However, it was at that radio station, WBFO Public Radio in Buffalo, NY, that I first found work that excited me. At the time, the station was a buzzing experiment in live on-air and recorded music of all genres and innovative public affairs programming, with a few paid but many volunteer program hosts. It was the first Buffalo station to air NPR's *All Things Considered* (ATC), which had been created by a former WBFO leader who took the concept to NPR in D.C., using the Canadian Broadcasting Corporation's "As It Happens" daily news program as a model. I began working at WBFO as a volunteer in the promotion area, writing press releases and helping to write and produce the monthly program guide. Soon I was hired part-time, and I took over the promotion director's role when she moved out of state. But I also started producing news and public affairs programs on an unpaid basis and did some freelance reporting for NPR out of the station.

At that time, the U.S. steel and auto industries were first sent reeling by a set of global forces that permanently altered the American economy. I reported on the massive changes that cutbacks in industrial production prompted in the finances of Buffalo and Lackawanna and the lives of Western New York residents. It was a dreary introduction to the dismal science of economics, but its impact was so deep and widespread that it left me with an abiding interest in business and economics reporting.

During 1978, I produced two hour-long programs at WBFO that were accepted for national broadcast by National Public Radio – the first was OPTIONS: Steel Import Quotas – Needed or Not? The second addressed another area in which massive change was occurring in the American economy and raising fundamental questions about our society – OPTIONS: Women and Work.

After producing those documentaries, I wrote a successful women's training grant proposal to the Corporation for Public Broadcasting to fund my salary for one year as a business reporter and economic affairs producer for WBFO. As part of the project, I completed two post-graduate courses in economics at the University at Buffalo. Between December 1978 and December 1979, I also produced, wrote, and hosted two weekly programs – Money Matters, broadcast during the station's daily "magazine" show, and Dollars and Change in Western New York, featuring a half-hour of live guests, call-ins, or produced documentaries. The two programs covered a wide range of topics, including the effect of the federal budget on the city of Buffalo; the role of taxes in the economy; occupational safety; displaced homemakers; utilities and consumers; and the decline of Buffalo's industrial base. By December 1979, NPR's OPTIONS series had aired several other hour-long programs I'd produced, including an edited lecture by economic philosopher Robert Heilbroner and a highly produced documentary on Small Business.

On a personal level, the feminist movement of that decade made me reluctant to get legally married, although I had been in a committed monogamous relationship with one man for nearly seven years. Disinclined to become dependent, aware of the high divorce rate, desiring to be treated as an individual on my own terms rather than as an appendage to a husband, I remained legally single from early 1973 through late November 1979. But by the late autumn of 1979, we decided it was time for our families to meet, to celebrate our love, and make our commitment official before we headed from Buffalo to new life adventures in Chicago.

We wrote our own wedding vows and got married by a Justice of the Peace at the Roycroft Inn in East Aurora, New York on the Saturday after Thanksgiving in 1979. After the brief ceremony and dinner, we shared an open bar with our guests and listened to music from a local band with a fabulous clarinetist called Dr. Jazz who inspired a joyful evening of dancing.

I had supported my beau through law school. I felt it was time for him to back me up in my decision to become a freelance writer and journalist.

PIECES,
FOLLOWING 2010 RETROSPECTIVE,
WRITTEN BETWEEN 1970 - 1979

The Research Psychiatrist's Subject: A Memoir
(2010 retrospective on 1969-70)

One night during the late fall of my senior year in 1969, my anger about the state of my world boiled over. At school, I had an argument over Vietnam with a classmate who was the son of an Air Force officer. Before dinner, my father berated my mother over a bookkeeping error she had made at their store. Then, during dinner, when I tried to talk about my college plans, my father kept shushing me to hear a TV newsman say how many Vietnamese we had killed and what was wrong with my generation. At that point, I slammed my fork down, got up, walked around the table, and kicked the TV set. Without turning back, I ran to my room and slammed the door.

The girl inside me who had once done her best to cheer up my mother, to give her an affectionate pat, to help her in the kitchen while her husband criticized her relentlessly – that girl now shut her out. "I just want to be left alone," I said.

This is probably when my mom began comparing me to her older sister Leona, who had been sent to a mental institution at the age of 19. Leona began having "spells" soon after puberty, and they became more aggravated over time. By the time my mother was about 11 years old, Leona had grown so disturbed that she heard voices telling her to kill my mother. My grandmother found her with a sharp kitchen knife, heading to my mother's bedroom. At that point, my grandparents decided they had no choice but to send Leona away. I learned of my aunt's existence only when she died in 1963 – allegedly from exposure after escaping from Willard State Hospital in upstate New York.

By the summer of 1969, Aunt Leona was the furthest thing from my mind. My faith in God and country had waivered after television news broadcasts delivered a string of political assassinations, brutal beatings of Black protestors, and grotesque massacres of Vietnamese children into my living room, night after night. My Church, despite its doctrine of just war, had not taken a stand against U.S. involvement in Vietnam. In addition, I couldn't understand why women were not allowed to become priests.

Further shattered by a break-up with my first love, I began "acting out" like throngs of young people in the U.S. did at the time. From being a devout obedient Catholic girl who aced every test, displayed happy energetic school spirit, and firmly defended my virginity, I became a nascent hippie dabbling in pot and hallucinogens, experimenting with sex, and allowing nagging doubts about the divinity of Jesus to be overwhelmed by agnosticism.

Writing about these exploits in a diary, I did what adolescents do. I gave no thought to the possible consequences and left the diary out where my parents could easily find and read it.

Christmas vacation during my senior year in high school had just begun when my mother walked into my bedroom. "Your father and I have something we want to talk to you about," she said. She led me to the dining room, where my father was seated at the usual "head of the table" seat. When I looked down and saw my diary on the table, my heart started to race, my face grew hot, and my legs seemed paralyzed.

"You left this out on your dresser, and we are very concerned about what's in it," she began.

"How could you read my diary? It's private. You wouldn't understand what's in it."

My father interjected, "Oh I think we can understand some of it."

I thought about the entries in my diary telling what it felt like to smoke pot for the first time and how I had finally lost my virginity. I also knew that my efforts to evoke a muse to write poetry would appear to my mother and father as incoherent scrawls.

"We don't understand what's been happening to you. We're afraid you're doing things where you'll end up hurting yourself. We went to talk to the guidance office at school for help."

I thought silently, you didn't come to me first to ask me questions. You didn't suggest that I go with you to the guidance office. You didn't really talk to me at all until now.

The principal of Rome Catholic High School was a conservative Papist and a former Marine chaplain. The guidance officer was another former military man. I was an opponent of the Vietnam War in a town with an Air Force base and I had openly questioned Catholic doctrine about guardian angels in my daily religion class. My parents had turned to the advocates of conservative Catholicism and U.S. military intervention for advice about how to deal with behavior they had never seen in their other children.

"Father Morelle gave us the name of a doctor and we went to see him," my mother continued.

"What kind of doctor?" I asked.

"A psychiatrist who takes care of the nuns when they need counseling. The doctor says you've been using drugs that are laced with some damaging chemicals, and he gave us a prescription for medicine that will counter the effects."

How did this doctor know what drugs I had taken? I had never even met the man.

"Why does he think that?"

"We showed him your diary. He knows what kind of drugs have been circulating. You need to start taking this medicine to avoid damage they can cause."

My mother handed me a large brown vial of prescription medicine labeled "Trilafon." I didn't know what it was, but I knew that if I refused to take it, I could end up like my friend's mother who was sent to Marcy for electroshock when she refused to take her meds. By the age of 17 in the era of civil rights battles, anti-war protests, and political assassinations, I had learned that the punishment only gets more severe for those who don't cooperate.

The pills were round, with a hard, shiny gray coating. I took four per day. As current pharmaceutical images would indicate, these were 16 milligram tablets, which means I was taking 64 milligrams of Trilafon, called perphenazine in the generic form, per day. Within days, I felt and looked like a zombie. I could not laugh, smile, cry, or change the tenor of my voice. In psychological terms, my affect was flat as the surface of a Texas highway.

After taking this medication for two weeks during Christmas vacation, my parents sat down with me once again in the dining room. "The doctor says that it would be best if you were in the hospital now," my mother said, "St. Elizabeth's Hospital in Utica can take you in today. You'll need to pack some clothes."

I had read Ken Kesey's *One Flew Over the Cuckoo's Nest*. It was a badge of courage in those years to be sent away against your will, and I knew it was common for creative, countercultural people to be considered crazy. But these were my parents. My mom and dad had suddenly decided that whatever I said was suspect, and whatever this doctor said was gospel truth.

When I got to the hospital Psychiatric ward, I saw Charlie who spent hours shuffling cards, laying them out for solitaire, and then picking them up again without ever playing the hand he had dealt himself. There was Katharine, about two years older than me, who would imagine voices and sights that were not there, an experience I had never encountered. And Gertrude, a small older woman constantly asked everyone she encountered, "Do you have any cigarettes? Can you get me a cigarette?"

I was left alone in a room with two beds. I had brought with me Thomas Merton's *The Seven Storey Mountain*, and Walt Whitman's *Leaves of Grass*, my favorite collection of poetry. There was little to do but eat, walk around the ward, and read.

By the fourth day in the hospital, after taking the medication for nearly three weeks, I had still not yet met the doctor who prescribed the pills and sent me there. My eyesight was failing me. When I tried to read, the lines on the page quadrupled and blurred. Within another day, my small seventeen-year-old breasts, which had little sexual experience and certainly no experience with pregnancy, were oozing milk.

The following day, I finally had an appointment with the doctor, a tall man with graying dark hair and glasses. I was shocked to see that this was the same man who had addressed me and other high school students at a statewide junior leaders conference the year before. There, in a thickly accented speech, he gave a rambling talk we all found bizarre about animals in the jungle getting drunk from fermented fruit juice.

"Hello, I'm Doctor Sainz," he said.

Months later I learned that Dr. Sainz had already diagnosed me as an "undifferentiated schizophrenic" based solely on meeting my parents and reading my diary. I discovered quickly through firsthand experience that Trilafon acts like a chemical lobotomy, turning active human minds into catatonic bumps. Decades later, I found that the dosage prescribed to me then is now considered far too high even for a raving schizophrenic.

It was also decades before I understood that my diary and behavior had resurrected my mother's fears about her sister Leona. I believe she convinced herself that the mental illness that had banned her older sister to a state institution at the age of 19 had finally cropped up again in the youngest of her six children. The trust that my mom once had in me was shattered by memories of events that predated my birth by nearly 30 years, and by my own behaviors that were common during the countercultural 1960s, but that baffled and frightened Depression-era adults.

The salves of time and distance and support from key friends and family have soothed the anger, pain, and fear that resulted from these events. Subsequent good doctors – psychiatrists and psychologists – have assured me repeatedly that I am not, and never was, a schizophrenic. Long ago, I forgave my parents and myself for mistakes we made as a result of being misguided.

But I cannot forgive nor forget that a man in a white coat treated me like a white rat in a lab. I will never fully recover from his carelessness and the fact that he violated a core tenet of the Hippocratic oath: "First, do no harm."

Pieces written between 1970 — 1979
Salutatory Speech of Linda M. Wagner, age 17

June 1970 — Graduation Ceremony, Rome Catholic High School, Rome, New York, USA

My comments today are directed to my fellow classmates, my dearest friends.

From growing with all of you for the past four years, I know we are a class that loves good times. I warn you now that the future holds a world which threatens that fun, a world of repression, of division, of hatred, and of war. Yet I truly feel that we can hang on to our good times. How? By remaining as adolescents who will keep their dreams alive.

The world outside belongs to a generation from whose hands we will take the reins. We have been called nihilists and have been claimed to be ready to destroy a society which we cannot replace. Yet we know, as D. T. Suzuki says, that "negativism is sound as method, but the highest truth is an affirmation."

Our affirmation is freedom — freedom to be all that we are and hope to be. This kind of freedom does not flow from any external system but from within, from the heart. It is present, however stifled, in every society. Our generation in our country has a monopoly on this kind of freedom and we will put it to use.

As we meet the future, each of will exercise this freedom in a unique way. In so doing we will become part of a movement that is sweeping our nation. We have long been sheltered from this movement, but we now must encounter it face-to-face. It is the movement of a people that are vibrant with life and hope. It is a movement that believes that we can attain love, freedom, peace, and full life. It is a movement that achieves its goals through its very struggle to attain them. It is composed of people who look upon life with the fresh, hopeful outlook of children.

My hopes today are idealistic. They are the hopes of one who has not become embittered with the so-called reality of life. Not yet, that is. But do we ever need to accept this reality? Must we grow to a maturity in which our childlike hopes cannot be realized? Once we reach that maturity, we will stop striving, as millions before us have done.

Yes, I ask you to remain as children, for only then can you gain the kingdom of heaven. I ask you to remember as the years pass that life should be enjoyed. Don't blindly accept the so-called reality of life. Don't give up your dreams.

Aunt Leona (Whom, in a State Mental Hospital, I Never Met) Speaks for the First Amendment

Screaming
The world has abandoned me
    To brick walls and neutral colors
Mother, father, sisters, and brothers
    Have shoved me to a corner
Where chemical restraints and isolation barbs
    Are tied around my mind.

Screaming
    And pounding a drumbeat
    That their ears refuse to hear
My family pretends it bears no malice
    Feigns comfort
    But hates itself.

Screaming
I am in a cell
Barred and locked
    With no room to stretch my legs
I can't express free-flung joy
    In life and love,
    Pleasure or wondrous color!
I no longer feel what to express.
Not my fault

Screaming
    Not my fault
The crack in my psyche
    Is made from blood and sinew,
    Bone and muscle
    Microcosmic family stuff
    Deep in my cellular center
You gave to me at birth

Screaming
    From generations of self-immolation
    Turned around
From centuries of anger and jealousy
    Stored in the chemical fluids
    That bathe the tissues of my brain.

Screaming
I have a right to exist
    And be and look like me
I have a right to dream big dreams
    Feel stormy nights and placid days
That the world foists upon my senses
I have a right
Screaming
I have a right to scream.

Post Rape

Tanning butter covers me
Head to foot,
A thin film between me and the sun.
Eyes closed, I listen.
Waves crash at the shore.
Seagulls call from the sky.
People gather at the beach,
Shuffling by, raising sand.
Morning passes.

A friend sleeps still
Beside me
She forgets
The sleep we lost the night before.
The noises melt together,
I fall asleep
Under strong rays of sun,

Only to awaken, startled,
Feel the heat penetrating every pore.
I leave the beach,
The roads of Florida, Alabama, Georgia,
Interstates 4 and 75,
Return to the cold
Northern climate where
Civilized newscasts relate remote tales
Of murder, theft, rape,
And the rising cost of food.

Now I feel my crusted face,
Peel the burnt skin from my forehead,
Leaving it red
And sore.

Early May 1973 - A First Person, Plural, Has Begun

You were on the other side of the waterfall –
Our fingers met inside the rushing water
Which, for all its force, could not break our touch apart.
Sunlight formed a rainbow in the spray
Then suddenly, trails cut through jungle branches
Leading to drier climates
A tear fell
Bursting with drops of laughter
Shedding pains and joys of past years
Within the ecstasy of holding hands
As we stood at the mountain top,
Facing the wide expanse of blue above us.

May 30, 1973 - For Barry

Sweetly you kissed
The zone in which my feeling
Becomes real to me
And where there is no desire
To escape.
As you felt my feelings
I came
To the realization
That love (unlike so much of what is real) is
What I think it should be.

Moral and Political Decisions on Abortion (1974)

(College Essay for Ethics Course)

INTRODUCTION

The topic of abortion provokes a host of legal and moral questions today across the world. It is not a typical political issue for these questions directly evoke our most fundamental conceptions of human life, civilization, and the future of the human race. The questions which have arisen and have been voiced about abortion illustrate that it is an issue whose "solution" has serious and widespread implications for the moral, legal, and political directions of American society and perhaps of world society.

The legal question of abortion in the United States was supposedly settled by a Supreme Court decision in January 1973, in which it ruled that "until approximately the end of the first twelve weeks of pregnancy, abortion is a decision that rests between a woman and her physician." [i] Helene S. Arnstein, in *What Every Woman Needs to Know About Abortion*, says:

> The Supreme Court's ruling on abortion was the culmination of a change in medical, philosophical, sociological, psychological, religious, and moral attitudes that had been taking place for some time. [ii]

She goes on to attribute this change to "social forces which dramatically swayed public opinion," including relaxed sexual mores, the high cost of welfare programs, overpopulation, the influence of the women's movement, medical progress, and concern for the unwanted child. [iii]

---

i   Helene S. Arnstein, *What Every Woman Needs to Know About Abortion*, Charles Scribners's Sons, New York, 1973, p. 25.

ii   Ibid., p. 21.

iii   Ibid., p. 21-25.

However, the issue has not, in fact, been settled. A significant number of constitutional amendments have been proposed in the Senate and House of Representatives, some of which would redefine the word "person" as it appears in the Fourteenth Amendment to include the human fetus, and would, in effect, guarantee equal protection and due process to the fetus. Other proposed amendments would return the abortion question to the domain of state legislation. Russell Shaw in *Abortion on Trial* admits that the law cannot settle the question of whether the fetus is, "in fact a person," but adds:

> The law must, however, make a determination in the matter for its own purposes, and its determination is obviously highly relevant in deciding whether proposed abortion liberalization statutes are consistent with legal doctrine.[iv]

The legislatures cannot appeal to conclusive biological evidence that human life begins at a certain point in the development of a human fetus, for there is none. In making its "determination," it seems likely that the law will appeal to, or rely on, public opinion in this matter. In other words, the legal questions of abortion in the United States may be finally decided directly by the popular morality held by the majority of American voters; thus, the centrality of discussing the moral issue of abortion.

It is important to realize that the moral questions raised when deciding on abortion policy seem to fall into two categories which may or may not be logically, or even psychologically connected. The first category is the morality of the individual action of abortion; the second is the morality of an explicit legal policy about abortion, whether it is a liberal policy or a restrictive one. These two cannot be treated as completely separate from each other. A decision about the morality of the individual action of abortion plays a fundamental part in the decision of a legal policy about abortion. However, they should be separated as clearly as possible when analyzing the moral character and the moral, political, and social consequences of adopting a policy on abortion.

---

iv   Russell Shaw, *Abortion on Trial*, Pflaum Press, Dayton, Ohio, 1968, p. 63.

Let us treat the moral problem of abortion as three separate questions: 1) When does human life begin?[v]; 2) Whether or not we consider the fetus to be a human life, under what circumstances, if any, are we justified in destroying it?; 3) Under what conditions should we allow abortions in the legal policy we adopt? The first two questions are concerned centrally with the first category mentioned above, the morality of the individual act of abortion. The third question is concerned with the second category, the morality of an explicit legal abortion policy.

I will try here to present the answers which are given to these questions by two groups of people who address them: first, those "right to life" proponents who would prohibit abortion under any circumstances; second, those right to abortion proponents who would consider abortion to be justified when performed to ensure the physical, mental, and/or socioeconomic health of the mother (or family) involved. For purposes of simplification, I will call the first view the conservative view and the second the liberal view.

I

The conservative claims that human life begins at the moment of conception when the genotype of an individual human being is determined. This claim is made despite the fact that it is not scientifically verifiable. As Helene Arnstein says:

> Philosophical, medical, and religious debate over when life begins has been going on for centuries. Life is certainly present in the fertilized egg and even in the unfertilized egg, but no one as yet has been able to determine at what point an embryo or fetus should be regarded as a human being or a member of society.[vi]

Journalist David Lowe concluded that:

---

v   Roger Wertheimer, in his essay "Understanding the Abortion Argument," in *Philosophy and Public Affairs*, Vol. 1, No. 1, Fall, 1971, discusses this formulation of the abortion question.
vi   Helene S. Arnstein, p. 16.

The decision as to what is human and deserves the rights accorded to humans and what is not and doesn't deserve those rights is simply not a decision that Science can make; it is a fundamental moral decision.[vii]

That abortion is the unjustifiable murder of an innocent human being is a position that, for the conservative, is totally resistant to further consideration. Roger Wertheimer, in "understanding the Abortion Argument," says that in being "stuck with the indeterminateness of the fetus's humanity...whatever you believe, it's not true – but neither is it false. You believe it and that's the end of the matter."[viii]

The first question of the morality of abortion is thus answered unequivocally by the conservative. While there seems to be more room for debate in the second question, and although some conservatives answer it differently from others, the most consistent conservative view offers this answer: Under no circumstances and at no time can abortion be justified. The conservative believes that a fetus is a human life from the moment of conception. But he believes further that the life of an innocent human being may never be taken. Innocent human beings have an absolute right not to be killed by another human being. And a fetus is clearly an innocent human being. Abortion is always murder and "murder is against the natural law."[ix] Wertheimer explains that, to the Catholic (in this case, the conservative),

> The issue is not, as the liberal supposes, one of religious ritual and self-regarding behavior, but of minority rights, the minority being not Catholics but the fetuses of all faiths, and the right being the right of an innocent human being to life itself.[x]

This position, that to abort a fetus is murder, is a moral decision about the morality of the individual action of abortion, which was called above the first category of the moral questions concerning abortion policy. Conservatives

---

vii   David Lowe, *Abortion and the Law*, Pocket Books, 1966, p. 73.
viii   Roger Wertheimer, p. 88-89.
ix   David Lowe is quoting obstetrician Dr. Roy Heffernan, p. 68.
x   Roger Wertheimer, p. 73.

seem to view this position as logically connected with questions in the second category, i.e., the morality of an explicit legal policy on abortion, in this case, a restrictive policy. What is this connection and how is it explained?

Russell Shaw speaks from the conservative viewpoint on this issue:

> The real question is not whether laws reflect someone's idea of right and wrong, but whether they serve the common good of society... (whether) they protect the key societal principle that innocent life may not be directly attacked – not on grounds of convenience, nor relief of hardship, nor even what appears to be necessity.... This surely is a principle whose protection is not only in the best interests of society but is essential to the continued existence of civilized society.[xi]

The conservative rejects a liberalized legal policy on abortion because he/she/they views such a policy as defeating the purpose of a legal order. A brief sketch of the conservative argument which illustrates the connection between its answers to the first category and the second category of the morality of abortion may be helpful in making this point clearer:

> First category: Human life begins at the moment of conception. Therefore, a fetus is a human being (human life) at every stage of its development after conception.
>
> The destruction of innocent human life for any reason is murder. Abortion is the destruction of innocent human life.
>
> Therefore, abortion is murder, and unjustifiable.
>
> Second category: The protection under law of innocent human life (protection against murder) is a principle on which the existence of civilized society is founded. Legalizing abortion is legalizing murder. Thus, legalizing abortion undermines the foundation of civilized society.

---

xi   Russell Shaw, p. 68-69.

Shaw points out that "...if innocent life may legally be attacked directly in one case, it is at best difficult to argue convincingly that it may not be attacked in another."[xii] Wertheimer approaches this point through the use of a startling comparison.

> The tragedies brought on by unwanted children are plentiful and serious – but so too are those brought on by unwanted parents, yet few liberals would legalize patricide as the final solution to the massive social problem of the permanently visiting parent who drains his children's financial and emotional resources.[xiii]

Yet it is just such a trend of solutions which the conservative fears as consequences of liberalizing abortion laws. Shaw quotes Julian Pleasant's article, "A Morality of Consequences":

> How does our attitude toward everyone change if we judge a person's right to life by what his life does to our plans?[xiv]

Pleasant claims that "our whole social fabric" is "placed in jeopardy" by such judgments.

When presented as such, it becomes clear that very fundamental moral issues are at stake to the conservative regarding the moral question of abortion. The very preservation of civilization is at stake to the conservative. Clearly, such a view cannot be taken lightly, especially when founded upon premises that are not clearly wrong to many people.

However, if the premises of the conservative argument are not clearly wrong, then they also are not clearly right. This is, of course, the source of the difficulty involved with the abortion issue. Let us turn to the liberal answers to the three questions stated above: when human life begins; when, if ever, it is justifiable to destroy the fetus; and what conditions for allowing abortion we should admit into a legal policy about it.

---

xii   Shaw, p. 43
xiii   Wertheimer, p. 72.
xiv   Shaw quotes Pleasant, p. 123.

II

Little of the literature proposing liberal views on abortion concerns itself directly with the question of whether the fetus is actually a human life or not. Largely, the liberal viewpoint admits more readily than the conservative the present impossibility of determining conclusively when human life begins. However, many hold the view of psychiatrist, Dr. John Cotton:

> ...I feel that most of us today think that in the early weeks of pregnancy, before you have a viable human being that can survive on its own, that abortion is not murder, and that one has a perfectly reasonable right, and, I almost feel, a duty to concern oneself with the health of a pregnant woman – her total health.[xv]

A more radical statement of this view is given by feminists Caroline Lund and Cindy Jaquith.

> The charge that abortion equals murder is demagoguery. A fetus is no more a human being than an acorn is an oak tree. The emotion-laden word 'murder' is used to obscure the real issues involved: the rights, the safety, and the whole course of life of pregnant women. It is absurd to equate the 'rights' of the fetus to the rights of a pregnant woman.[xvi]

Regarding the fetus as a "potential human life" rather than an actual human life, the liberal holds the view that the fetus need not be accorded full human rights, especially when they conflict with the rights of the pregnant woman, e.g., the right to decide when to have children. The liberal argument does not confront the conservative view directly by attempting to demonstrate that the fetus is not to be regarded as living or as human. Rather, it regards these questions as insoluble or irrelevant. The reason seems to be that it is the welfare, not simply the life, of the 'potential' human being within the fetus, that concerns the liberal.

---

xv   Lowe is quoting Dr. Cotton, p. 72.
xvi   Caroline Lund and Cindy Jaquith, Abortion on Demand: A Woman's Right, Pathfinder Press, inc., New York, 1971, p. 8.

Dr. Alan Guttmacher, chair of Planned Parenthood World Population, points out, "There is so much more to life than simply a beating heart and a breathing lung." Concerned with the mother's right to health, he adds that health should be interpreted "broadly," as by the World Health Organization (WHO): "Health is a state of complete physical, mental, and social well-being, not simply the absence of illness and disease."[xvii] The liberal points to the empirical consequences of restrictive abortion laws: mental anguish of women discovering an unwanted pregnancy, the deaths and injuries produced in illegal abortions, the inequity of restrictive laws (a rich woman can get an abortion whenever she wants one), the physical and emotional strain of pregnancy, the financial and social difficulties of raising "one more child," and notably, the problem of unwanted children.

We see that the liberal answers the first two questions of the morality of abortion as follows: 1) We cannot be certain when human life begins; and 2) We are justified in terminating a human pregnancy (until approximately the third to sixth month of pregnancy) when the physical, mental, or socioeconomic health of the mother or family is seriously endangered by the pregnancy. (These conditions should be seriously considered by the woman.)

The conservative answer to question three is, quite simply, that we should admit no conditions for allowing abortion into our legal policy. The liberal answer to this question is understandably more complicated. It seems to me that the basic liberal approach here aims at improving the existing 'civilized' society, while the conservative approach claims to be one of preserving the existing civilized society.

The conditions under which abortions are morally allowable to the liberal are the conditions under which abortions should be legally allowable; the conditions are justifiable by the premise that society will benefit by granting women the right of deciding when she wants to bear her children. An attempt is being made to guarantee the welfare of mothers and the welfare of society's future children, and thus, to guarantee the future welfare of the whole society. The

---

xvii   Lowe quotes Dr. Guttmacher, p. 60-61.

liberal considers that any abortion is unfortunate, but also that it is an action which is called for in many cases in response to practical moral responsibilities. We have empirical evidence of the consequences of unwanted pregnancies where abortion is prohibited; we have no empirical evidence to support the claim that abortion is murder. A flexible legal policy allowing abortion under some circumstances is justified by the need to alleviate the present difficulties in society of unwanted pregnancies and to allow for an improved, more humane society, according to the liberal.

III

The insistence was made in this paper's introduction that the moral questions of abortion be separated into two categories because of the timeliness of the issue of abortion as a legal question. American society must decide on a policy on abortion to be upheld by American law. The answers that the conservative view and liberal view give concerning the second category, i.e. the morality of an explicit legal policy on abortion, point out basic differences between them in their attitudes toward the purpose of a legal order or of civilization.

The conservative sees legal abortion as legal murder, a threat to the continued existence of the existing civilization. The liberal sees legal abortion as a gateway to a more humane society, a more humane civilization. Using Lon Fuller's language, the conservative emphasizes "order" as the purpose of a legal system; the liberal emphasizes "good order."

The reaction of Ms. Lund and Ms. Jaquith noted above to the conservative view that abortion is murder is too simplistic and displays a misunderstanding of the gravity of the conservative view. Patrick J. Coffey gives a warning in his essay, "Toward a Sound Moral Policy on Abortion:"

> It may well be that much of the argument favoring a liberal moral policy on abortion for our society is based not upon what is morally right but rather upon what is at best sometimes morally excusable. A practice of this sort may in fact alleviate the distressing side-effect of injustice suffered by a pregnant mother who will be

morally blameless in her action of abortion. But it would not be a just practice, and, furthermore, it would actually reinforce moral behavior by permitting, if not tacitly encouraging, society to continue evading its responsibility to make alternatives to abortion more available.[xviii]

I would question the validity of Coffey's accusation. There are many "liberals" who clamor for childcare services, minimum family allowances, more jobs, and better institutions for the mentally ill and those with intellectual and physical disabilities. *(Addendum: In addition, liberals have often supported, above conservative opposition, improvements in sex education, the availability of birth control, and laws regarding rape and incest, since rape, including spousal rape, and incest often result in unwanted pregnancies.)*

Nevertheless, the points that Coffey and Shaw make should be carefully considered. The abortion question has arisen partly because so few social and legal measures are taken to avoid the need for abortion.

On the other hand, many conservatives claim that women seeking abortions are acting without conscience out of a desire for mere expedience or convenience. This attitude is also unjustly oversimplified. While it is true that a liberal law on abortion may be abused by some women merely for their convenience, such abuse does not follow from the law but from the attitudes of these few women. I must strongly contend here that most women who are faced with the choice about abortion seriously consider that choice and are most often faced with <u>other moral responsibilities</u> that conflict significantly with that of bearing a child. It is these women alone who must directly confront the moral question of the individual act of abortion. Since the fetus is within their wombs, the final responsibility of the individual abortion lies with them. To disregard their feelings and thoughts is to beg the moral question in a very fundamental sense. David Lowe speaks of the doctors confronted by these women:

---

xviii Patrick J. Coffey, "Toward a Sound Moral Policy on Abortion," in *The New Scholasticism*, Vol. XLVII, No. 1, Winter, 1973, p. 112.

Because they are not philosophers or moralists, they are not much given to wide generalizations. What they want is to prevent the suffering of the women they see every day in their offices. When doctors talk about abortions, they are most likely to draw from their own experiences, and it is worthwhile to pay attention to these experiences. For, in the end, this is the actual situation to which lawmakers and clergy must give heed when they come to generalize about what ought to be done and why.[xix]

When deciding on the adoption of a legal policy on abortion, we must address the question of the morality of such a policy. When addressing this question, we must consider the question of the morality of <u>any</u> legal policy. Roger Wertheimer has pointed out that our interactions with fetuses are extremely limited.[xx] Thus, the legal concept of a person is very difficult to apply to the fetus. How can the state justify legal prohibitions against abortions while the answer to the question, "When does human life begin?" remains a moral choice? The Supreme Court decision in Roe v. Wade seems to be an adequate response to the pressing need for abortion reform. But it does not solve the moral questions of individual acts of abortion; the individual must answer them for herself or himself.

However, the question of legal policy regarding abortion is a concern of the whole society. The time will probably arrive soon when our present liberal abortion policy will be re-evaluated by the legislatures. I suggest that the prime source of information in such an evaluation should be requested from women who have had to face the moral question of abortion individually and have decided either in favor or against abortion. Only by investigating the needs of these individual women can we discover the needs of society in dealing with the problem of unwanted pregnancy. It is these needs that should determine most clearly what policy is moral, or as Russell Shaw put it, which policy is in the service of "the common good of society."

---

xix   Lowe, p. 58.

xx   Wertheimer discusses this point toward the end of his article.

Seeing the USA in our Dodge Dart

We hiked near streams, rivers, lakes oceans,
Climbed hills and mountains, gorges, caves, and canyons,
Ate mangoes, Bing cherries, shrimp, and tacos,
And saw spring, summer, and winter.
But where is autumn?
Yet to come autumn, with rich colors and fragrant crispness,
Holding a silent song more peaceful
Than the call of evening birds in mountain woods.

Where the animals go
So goes the human
And we still see the rise and fall and rise again
Of hundreds, even thousands of suns, moons, stars.
But it is in this place and time
Hearing the shortness of breath of an imagined dying child
In my mind's ears,
That I can no longer bear the thought of living
Within such a world as I am today.

The bombs and planes and radar,
The missiles and biological weapons,
The nuclear waste seeping into water, wind, and soil,
The industry grinding out plastic, metal, and exhausted people,
The cars, buses, trains, planes, and motorcycles,
The clangs, crashes, and buzzing hum,
The anger in the voices of old and young.

The human - and my - need to be a Renaissance woman
Four centuries too late and long ago,
Fulfillment far from our memories,
The living, dying, learning, loving,
And even the hating.

There is so much work to be done
For everything and everyone.

Setting out

To lose the vantage point of having an occupation, which makes you "be something" – and of living in a place, which makes you "from somewhere" – you must exert more effort to find who you really are, the you with whom you feel most comfortable.

I don't quite know how to relate to myself. I don't feel that what I'm doing is wrong or stupid or foolish. And yet something about it seems unusual to me. I'm surprised that it isn't really freaking me out.

Living your life is a series of situations. You can do a lot of things with your life. And I have such a great number of possibilities. I'm young, healthy, with friends and family who love me.

Living your life actively in the moment however – it is a peculiar situation that few people have the opportunity to experience. Tied to no jobs, no school, no place – committed only to a relationship that is important, that I wish to maintain and develop.

Sharing freedom.

Mount Lassen Love Poem

Mid-June 1975

Volcano erupted inside me
Twice this afternoon
In Little Green Mount Marcy tent
By Manzanita Creek
Rushing rapidly past
Like blood through my body
And hormones through my blood.
Laughter in my voice
From deep within
The happy me that you reach
With your Semite sense of humor and gentility
And your warm touching my everywhere
With your everywhere.
Outside there's no one else
Rising with only our sneakers on
No need to worry or be afraid
In the wilderness
Uninhabited by our "fellow man"
Who will hunt and kill his own kind
Even with food all around him
Unlike other animals.

But let's be kind and forget
How did those impulses come
To our species?
We cannot know
Here with mountains across from us
Snow, setting sun, cool evening air,
Steady sound of moving water
No one else around
Just you and I...

Can I Sell You My Words?

June 1975

Will you buy my art
From me
Take it away – it's no good here
In the mountains, tucked away
Children nearby playing and hiding
From each other and their elders
Sun still setting? No, it's gone.
Overhead a plane rumbles
Words don't do – just to listen
To a frog or a rustle in the bushes
Where rabbits move through,
Running from hawks circling above
Not now though – the sun is gone
I can barely see the page
Words are not clear to me
But the quiet of an outdoor night
Here it makes me feel secure
Even though I have no home.

When the Party is Over:
Ruminations After My 1975 USA Travel Adventure

Part I

My boyfriend and I worked at low-skilled jobs just before and after we graduated from college, to get enough money to do something we really wanted to do – travel around the United States. We wanted the leisure time to enjoy each other, the excitement of seeing new places and meeting new people, the education of looking at this entire large country into which we were born and raised.

In some ways, to some people, it was a poor investment for our future. Now our money is gone, and we are again working at low-paying, low-skilled jobs, far away from friends and most of our family. Like so many other Americans, we must move around to get ahead, and start from scratch all over again.

We traveled in a slant-six Dodge Dart, camping out and staying with relatives, from Buffalo south to Florida, across Louisiana and Texas to southern California and up the West Coast highway to Eugene, Oregon, and then back over the Rocky Mountains, to the Grand Canyon, and much more, landing in Lexington, Kentucky. We took photos on a Kodak instamatic, the 126x. We rode the cable cars in San Francisco and discovered they actually had signs for Rice-A-Roni on the backs of the cars.

During that trip in 1975, I noticed many things that were different from the world in which I grew up.

- Changing roles of the family, including women loving women and men loving men and establishing homes together, evident in San Francisco

- How changing yourself can imply changing your behavior OR changing your attitudes, and how changing our attitudes can result in behavioral changes

- That condominiums or other planned housing with rules about who can live in or even visit planned communities is segregating the middle class by age and family status

- In the cities, there was a trend toward murals on the sides of buildings

- An overwhelming diversity of interest groups

- Localities or regions were focused on issues that had national import but only local awareness, such as

  o The Attica inmate trials in Buffalo;

  o The reclaiming of the inner city by the wealthy in Philadelphia;

  o Castro's Cuba in the news in Florida but not evident elsewhere;

  o Throughout the deep South, we heard about the trial of Joan Little, an African American woman jailed for breaking and entering, whose defense for killing a jail guard in Wake County, North Carolina, was that she was defending herself against sexual assault (In August 1975, Little was acquitted by a jury of Black and white men and women.)

- Natural flows of water are being diverted by a variety of local, state, federal forces, and a range of business interests, including corporate agribusinesses.

- The USA rests on an underlying continental plate that can move, break, and split.

- Americans are plagued with self-doubt.

- Signs of climate change are everywhere.

It was so clear that there are vast differences between occurrences that are natural and those that are man-made. It felt frightening that we have tampered so much with the wilderness that we have made ourselves increasingly subject to its changes, not less so. Our society's framework is top-heavy. The complex of corporate-military-industrial-bureaucratic institutions still rest on the crust of the earth. Everywhere we traveled, people noted significant changes in their local weather in recent years. We found so many examples of radical changes in natural phenomena, whether due to lumber companies, oil companies, corporate agriculture, the U.S. Army Corps of Engineers or local or state agencies that it seemed feasible that weather changes could be occurring because of human interferences in natural processes. For example, we learned that water from the Colorado River that once flowed to Northern Mexico has been diverted for crop irrigation in California. Aside from the international political ramifications of such an act, the man-made removal of large natural flows of water to another location must eventually change weather patterns and geological processes in both areas.

Our society is in constant motion – the motion of cars every day, the motion of ideas and information that passes through our minds, the motion of the places we call home, the motion of shifting values. But many people in our society are less mobile and not ready to accept change. They are invested in what constitutes their lives now. They are reluctant to enjoy the appearance of novelty in their world. They are happy with the way things are for them and so, they fear change. Unfortunately, many of those orchestrating the rapid changes in our world have no regard for those fears and no interest in seeking to alleviate or compromise with them.

Part II

"In the cookie I read
some get the gravy
some get the gristle
some get the marrow bone
and some get nothing
though there's plenty to spare."

– Joni Mitchell (and the fortune cookie), "Banquet" released 1972

Our lives depend so much on the dollar and the work we must perform to gain it. Are we allowing ourselves to be totally defined by the economy and our places within it? Do we, the people of the USA, have anything else that is truly basic in our lives?

After getting my college degree and starting to work full time, I felt dissatisfied with everything, from cars to clothes, from jobs to schools, from movies to music. Did I have a simple case of Future Shock? Toffler, in his 1970 book, *Future Shock*, said we know what the future is going to be like: super-industrial, depersonalized, more mechanized, more affluent. I do feel alienated, less human, and confused by the masses of new knowledge pouring into my life. I feel rootless and lonely, as if the relationships that should be closest to me are too far away.

Toffler implied that we cannot change these trends; we must adapt. That's too much for me to swallow; I want to fight and change what he sees as inevitable. At the same time, I'm overwhelmed by the power plays in today's political world. Since Watergate broke, we've been deluged with revelations and admissions of struggles within and outside governmental and economic institutions. These struggles have involved the CIA, the Mafia, the President (and even the President's wife), Congress, city mayors, and courts charged with abuse of grand jury power.

Men as workers are pitted against women as feminists seeking jobs; adults as authority figures hover over children as small human actors; the leftist underground protests banks and corporations, and rich nations lord it over countries in the Third World. And that old favorite, "Communism against Capitalism," is still around, despite propaganda to the contrary.

Moreover, many power struggles in public and private spheres are fought with apparent disregard for their consequences. The Army Corps of Engineers moves rivers simply because they have the technology to conquer nature. Working class whites violently protest court-ordered busing that, they believe, takes school control out of their hands. Husbands and wives sleep with other men and women because they have the "right." The Armed Forces, allegedly in order to conquer foreign enemies, test LSD and disease organisms on their own troops. Some young Black teens terrorize old white people for the thrill of provoking fear. But many white cops stop young Black males for no reason other than to harass, beat, or even kill them. Members of an established middle-class live in condominiums in which they can control who and what is in their neighborhoods through a board of directors.

Should the world be viewed not as Toffler suggests in *Future Shock*, but rather as Nietzsche suggests in *Will to Power*? Is fulfillment of the human spirit only possible through control of the world's destiny? That seems to be madness, as it requires the loss of consideration for anything sacred, as if human life is valuable only as a means to our ends. As if the only thing that matters is that we can control someone, something, anything, or else our existence is simply a pile of inertia.

Why do most of us crave the feeling of control? Probably because we are so powerless in actuality. Power is most often tied to money. The more you have, the more control you have over your own life. And those who control the money itself have power not only their own lives, but over the lives of others. But must our lives hinge on money and the work we perform to gain it? Must we be defined by the economy and our places within it?

In the past, a good college education would give most graduates some say about the future of the world. But after earning my degree, I have read that its value has declined, and it will no longer assure me or other college grads upward social mobility. It appears that prior generations of college graduates earned more money, and in the realm of power, it was their money that did the talking, not their education. In fact, many of those who succeeded in business had no college degree. But because they had money, their power sometimes outstripped that of the college educated.

These days in the late 1970s, more and more of us have less and less of everything – money, jobs, security, permanence in relationships and place. We may feel the need to take greater risks, but we are fearful of losing what little we have. We will have to take the plunge, but what can we not risk losing?

My background in philosophy may show here like a lace slip below the hemline of a dress. Nevertheless, I propose that it is simply not worth the struggle for things in themselves - neither money nor power, fame nor security. Nothing IS in itself. All things in the world are related to each other, and people are more interdependent than ever.

We all have needs of our own, but we need each other as well, whether we are strong and honest enough with ourselves to admit it, or not. All of us – rich and poor, rulers and ruled, have ignored this fact far too long. The consequences have been disastrous.

To survive and thrive in our world, struggles for power must be motivated by love. Otherwise, when we grasp the results, they will run like sand between our fingers.

Subjugation of the Woman

December 1975

Telling her she is not as sexually attractive to you
As you pretended she was
When you first wanted to get between her legs
As conquest.
Turning her own anger at you
Against herself
To weaken her defenses
And make her your sexual prize.
Using your sexual attractiveness
To lure her into your lair
Then turning it off
And leaving her hungry.

How the Game is Rigged

Men do sports in groups
Against a lone theoretical female
Using sexual energy she arouses
To beat her at a game
That they define.

1976- 1979 Miscellaneous Buffalo Reflections

August 1976

Today's weather was gray. Cloudy skies trapped the odors of Lackawanna inside Erie County. A fine wet mist in the air chilled my bones.

I was walking home from Rob's Mobil station. My middle-aged, deteriorating Dodge Dart sat there getting its new universal join installed. I'm receiving $54 of unemployment insurance each week from New York State. My car repair bill will be $25 plus NYS sales tax. As I realized that this equals 11% of my monthly income, my neck muscles tensed up.

In Buffalo, I live on the edge of my existence. Here, an existentialist a la Jean Paul Sartre finds crystal clear contact with authentic Being (and Nothingness). The struggle is so real that dreamers cannot afford false expectations.

I am stuck inside the thrill of starkness, inside the center of a contradiction.

September 1976

The easiest way to keep people oppressed is by teaching them untruths. Confusion ensues when people know the truth of their experiences but are taught that what they know firsthand through their own senses is not the case. They lose faith in their own ability to see, hear and feel. They begin to mistrust their own senses and gut judgment. People who do not believe in themselves are easy to manipulate. To "lead" people in such a way is not true leadership. It is simple deception.

A true leader never needs to lie to his or her followers. A true leader's strength consists of the fact that he or she speaks the truth and speaks for the truth, and that the truth speaks through him or her.

When people recognize the truth of their own experience in the spoken or written words of a leader, then they are ready and willing to be led forward, because the faith they have in their leader is really faith in themselves.

September 1976

Putting together:

1. Labor force participation rates, with

2. Socioeconomic analysis of a capitalist society

Society in the USA is racist. It is becoming less sexist because the economy needs women working in order to expand. The economy does not yet need Blacks and other people of color. But it will, and it is planning for that eventuality. The white males have the affluence. Now, they allow white women to enter the labor force and earn money that gives them more leisure and flexibility. They can afford to be enlightened when it comes to women within their own caste.

There is more involved than economics. But if women's participation threatened the economic system, women's liberation would never have been possible. Those in power have seen the wisdom of being enlightened about women and work, women and credit, women and consumption at the right point for economic expansion.

Meanwhile, while white women are helping white men achieve more satisfaction in their lives, they are taking on new pressures and, in turn, leaving Blacks where they always were. The problem of racism becomes worse if Blacks aren't needed to expand the economy and reap profits for white men, with white women preferable to Black men or women. Because Blacks will remain out of the picture. The ghettos are perceived by those in power as a solution – keep the "full employment unemployment rate" centered in the Black population. They say, "Let Blacks bear the brunt of white flexibility and affluence."

Women are being used – their sexuality denied – their need to give life further devalued. Leave it to capitalism to do the "right" things for the wrong reasons.

October 17, 1976

Letter to "Morning Mail" in the *Buffalo Courier-Express* (Published)

Re: Articles on living together in Sunday, Oct. 17 Courier-Express

We've been living together unmarried for nearly three years. We love each other. We share household responsibilities, finances, and a commitment to respect each other.

We believe in the liberation of women and men from the sexist roles and property-obsession that marriage signifies to us. We aren't "thumbing our noses" at marriage. We simply see no need for its supposed "security" in our relationship.

We want our relationship itself to show that love does not rely on a piece of paper that says, "Your property is jointly owned." Marriage can't save people from a bad relationship when they don't know how to develop a good one. Over 50% of the marriages in the U.S. end in divorce – proof that a marriage ritual can't teach people how to love each other and live together happily.

Mr. Utts is right; living together isn't easy. Anyone who lives with other people knows that. But only the day-to-day, hard work struggle of love gives us meaning. Any marriage contract without it is just an empty symbol.

Our loving each other and living together are our symbols and our meaning. Who needs more security than that? I suggest that your writers stick to reporting news rather than telling us how to live our lives. You can't learn love from a newspaper article.

Sincerely,

Linda Wagner & Barry Ginsberg

Saturday, November 24, 1979 - Roycroft Inn, East Aurora, New York
Wedding Vows of Barry Ginsberg and Linda M. Wagner

Barry:

Thank you for coming to share and celebrate our marriage ceremony with us. This wedding is a public symbol of our feelings and commitment towards each other. Therefore, this occasion would not be possible without you.

Linda:

It is not for happiness alone that we marry. From our love, we draw strength. The bonds that marriage symbolizes give us hope and faith in humanity.

Barry:

We are not two halves combined to form a whole. We are two individuals joined in something as meaningful as our separate selves.

Linda:

In this ceremony the father of the bride will not give her away to the groom, as is traditional. We believe that the bride is neither the property of her father to give, nor of the groom to receive.

Barry:

I, Barry, take you, Linda, to be my wife, to live together in conformity with the laws of matrimony. I promise to love you, to honor you, to cherish you and to care for you in sickness and in health, in prosperity and adversity, so long as we both shall live.

Linda:

I, Linda, take you, Barry, to be my husband, to live together in conformity with the laws of matrimony. I promise to love you, to honor you, to cherish you and to care for you in sickness and in health, in prosperity and adversity, so long as we both shall live.

(Note to Justice of the Peace: Complete ceremony as usual, except please pronounce us husband and wife, and not man and wife.)

Even Nature Kills

1979

Did you think I didn't notice
That the virgin forest
Had several trees missing?
That only stumps remained
Where branches had been?
I saw the very men
Who stole into the woods
I saw them chop the living down.
I watched the whole thing happen.
Now you say
I didn't scream loud enough,
Didn't oppose
Didn't fight.
But I picked my battles
Fought them hard
And often won.
And those I didn't pick –
Well, they were lost.
There are hundreds of forests
Millions of trees
We pass them daily
And try to keep alive
The most we can.

But even nature kills,

Seasons change,

Leaves turn and die,

Fall from branches,

And branches fall from the trees.

The woods evolves.

I have some special trees

In the forests I know.

They are sturdy – some young, some old,

Some lovely in their symmetry

Some enchanting with complexity.

All beautiful in that they live,

Blossom green in spring

Turn rich colors with autumn

And retreat in the silence of winter

Only to grow again in spring.

I pass the time

With these trees

I know their shape and texture and names -

Cut them down and then,

You are my enemy.

Patriarchal Sophistication in a Capitalist Economy

Was it all a joke
That you should get me
To help you
Make more money
That my plans to
Change the world
Are gone
Evaporated into airwaves
And male technological
Advances
For centuries
Sayings have said
A woman is a fragile thing
You laugh
At the differences
You gave up trying
To understand
We feel as trapped
As ever
A higher level
Of sophisticated
Oppression
As isolated
From ourselves
As we have ever been

12/4/1979
Hostage Smiles on (U.S.) Presidents

I have been speculating about the roots of Islam, Shiite, Sunni, and Black Muslim. I'd like to know the answers to questions, but I'm afraid it's too late to ask.

As a woman, I know that religion can be oppressive. As a white American of European heritage, I know I am not part of it and alien to it. And that extremists would consider me Satanic.

When I was a child, I asked to speak with Satan. I asked for proof that Satan exists. I was a fool. I did not know the meaning of evil. But neither did I really know the meaning of love. Despite the fact that I was brought up in a religion of "love," the clergy did not teach me the meaning, except with abstractions and words.

But how does this apply to my life and the world today? Can I escape the violence of a "holy war?" It started years ago. I knew that something was out of sync.

Then I read "The Book." From a stranglehold of Western Catholic thought to the expansiveness of Eastern mysticism. From Christ the God/Man to Tao and Ying/Yang. And the balance of contradictions became the basis for my entirely new *weltanschauung*. I was able to understand what Buddhism and Taoism meant. And I was welcome to learn.

However, with Islam, I feel I have no place to start. I confronted Catholicism, Buddhism, and Judaism within my upbringing or personal contacts. But Islam – I have very little contact with or conception of it.

If someone were to ask me – what do you believe? What is your faith? This is how I would answer at this point in my life, at age 27:

I believe there is a spirit pool – that, at death, the "self" leaves the body, goes through a temporary phase like Limbo between this world and the next. And that the spirit then dissipates into Universal Spirit.

I believe there are connections between Universal Spirit and living human beings. Universal Spirit has all the accumulated knowledge and understanding of those who have died and dissipated into that Spirit. But there are times when the spirit of a living human being may merge with Universal Spirit – times of great enlightenment.

I suspect that those in Iran who proclaim a holy war may be of a different spirit pool. They are proclaiming a war to destroy the collective knowledge and understanding of a vast array of human spirit. I do not believe they can succeed. Perhaps they have not yet learned that we are really part of the same pool of energy.

Many people want to run from the wars that surround us daily. Iran was not a surprise to me. After all, what do these Western definitions of embassy and sovereignty mean to a people tortured by a leader that the U.S. government propped up in power for so long?

After all, the U.S. industries and government decided we needed oil to run our cars and boats all over God's country. What stupidity and absurdity.

Eleven young people are trampled to death at a rock concert. And people got more upset about our embassy in Iran? Our values seem upside down.

Linda while camping at Lassen Volcanic National Park in Northeast California, 1975

Linda Mary Wagner & Barry Ginsberg, circa 1978

DECADE II: 1980 - 1989

Full Adulthood & Motherhood: Age 28 - 37

A Struggle for Workers', Writers', and Parents' Rights

During the first half of the 1980s, I was between 27 and 32 years old and focused on becoming a professional writer and journalist. By the middle of the decade, my focus shifted to family matters, becoming a mother of two. During the latter 1980s, I found myself as one of six orphans of parents who were alive, but cognitively absent.

As newlyweds, Barry and I moved from Buffalo to Chicago in January 1980. After completing his law degree, Barry landed a clerkship at the federal district court in Chicago. I had fallen in love with radio and journalism after working at WBFO for three years, so I decided to focus my work life on free-lance journalism with National Public Radio and other clients. I began with a contract to research and write a *Kid's Guide to Chicago*, and a commitment from NPR that it would welcome story ideas as well as give me assignments, eased by my acquaintance with another WBFO alum, Jon "Smokey" Baer, who had been assigned as a producer by NPR to its new Chicago Bureau.

Between January 1980 and December 1982, I became a regular freelance contributor to *All Things Considered* and *Morning Edition* at NPR. I also did occasional work for CBC-Radio, Radio Smithsonian, the Bill of Rights Radio Education Project, G.L. Nelson Publishing Company, the *Chicago Reader*, *In These Times*, and several Chicago neighborhood newspapers. I produced two half-hour documentaries as part of the NPR JOURNAL series – "Parents' Rights'/Kids' Rights" and "Remembrance," a documentary about current scientific research into human memory, both of which were also distributed through NPR's annual cassette catalog.

At NPR's Chicago bureau in the early 1980s, I was fortunate to have such coworkers as NPR staff reporter Scott Simon, producer Jon Baer, engineer Rich Rarey and fellow freelancers at that time, including Jill Dougherty, Ina Jaffe, Alex Kotlowitz and Jacki Lyden. Our bureau also included political satirists and voice talent from Chicago's theater world as freelance contributors, including Warren Leming and others. My coverage of business stories was flavored by the Chicago-area economy, resulting in stories about the deregulation of the railroads and its impact on rural Illinois; the effect of droughts on commodities prices at the Board of Trade and at the supermarket; genetic engineering in agribusiness; minority-owned businesses; Sears's opening of financial service centers; retail trade during post-Thanksgiving Christmas sales; the introduction of cellular mobile phones; and a history of commercial shipping on the Great Lakes. In one of my favorite assignments, law, business, and labor reporting overlapped – the bribery trial of former Teamsters President Roy Williams. For nearly five months, I covered the story in-depth for NPR, and also filed for a news outlet called, at that time, Satellite News Channel.

In addition, I reported on a broad range of non-business stories, including some that had foreign policy implications. For example, I covered the successful family court efforts of a 12-year-old immigrant child named Walter Polovchak to remain in the U.S. after his father decided to return to his Ukrainian homeland, then under the Soviet Union. I interviewed South African poet Dennis Brutus, who put his gentle wordsmithing to work against his nation's apartheid regime after his release from prison there. I shared the story and music of Carlos Mejia Godoy, Nicaragua's foremost songwriter and folklorist, as he sang against the brutality of the U.S.-backed Contras and on behalf of the Sandinistas.

Some of my assignments were just plain fun, such as the reunion of the real women who had *A League of Their Own*, the players from the All-American Girls Professional Baseball League from 1943 – 1954. I covered some of the best drummers of the time at the 1983 Zildjian Day drumming festival;

enterprising female musicians at one of the National Women's Music Festivals in Bloomington, Indiana; and the cold-weather camping of a group of survivalists, many of whom had lost steel factory jobs and traveled on weekends from their homes in South Chicago to the hills of Wisconsin to prepare for the apocalypse they were certain was on its way 40 years ago.

In September 1982, my husband left his position as a federal law clerk. Before he started his next job at a high-pressure law firm, we decided to travel to France and England. We had the pleasure of staying with an elderly British couple in the East Anglia region of England, who had hosted my colleague Jacki when she was a student there. They warmed our bed with a hot water bottle and served us tea and biscuits by our bed in the morning. They insisted on taking us to see the rows and rows of white crosses in a nearby cemetery, where hundreds of Americans who fought in World War II were buried, to express their appreciation to our nation for supporting their fight against Hitler.

We took a train from England to Paris. We were fortunate again that an American friend, one of Barry's law colleagues, had arranged for us to stay briefly with a young Parisian couple. They were gracious to take us to an underground club to hear French jazz, to turn up the heat in their hot water for a more comfortable shower, introduce us to some of the best Burgundy wine and liqueur, and provide us with tourism tips. At the end of our stay in Paris, we rented bicycles, took the bikes and our backpacks aboard a train, and went south to the Loire Valley, where we rode from campsite to campsite and château to château. Some might say it was unwise to spend instead of saving, but the memories are worth every penny (or franc). I share stories of those travels in this section.

Traveling invigorated me as I returned to my freelance work. Most of my ideas, reports, and productions were accepted for broadcast. But unfortunately, my childhood shyness and anxiety often crippled me emotionally from believing that I could compete with the skills and egos of my coworkers. When my colleague Alex accepted a job with the *Wall Street Journal,* abandoning our joint documentary project on Prisoners' Rights and For-Profit Prisons, he said to me, "The difference between me and you is that I have an ego." In looking back, I can see that I should have had greater confidence in my own talents and abilities.

In 1983, NPR assigned me to follow the campaign of Harold Washington, who became the first Black person elected Mayor of the City of Chicago. I found it difficult to be unbiased; Washington promised to address issues about which my reporting on Chicago's Black community had made evident. Not long after the election, a fiscal crisis hit NPR, and I had to branch out further to freelance for numerous other news outlets. I edited and produced a series of recorded lectures on the world economy for the University of Chicago, provided research assistance to the BBC documentary series PANORAMA for their program "Called to Account" on the Calvi/Vatican Bank scandal, reported for AP Radio, and wrote for The *Chicago Tribune*'s regional sections.

In 1984, *The New York Times* regularly published a column titled "Hers." I submitted ideas and a sample. As so many writers find with so much of their hard work, those ideas were rejected. When a couple of other proposals fell flat, I found myself stuck in a mucky, demoralized phase, with the fragile confidence I had gained over the previous three years rapidly evaporating.

Throughout this period, the political environment in the U.S.A. was in flux. Democratic President Jimmy Carter had become unpopular in 1980 amid an energy crisis he had inherited and a hostage crisis in Iran that he was unable to negotiate. Ronald Reagan, who had gone from a grade B movie actor to an anti-Communist crusader to a conservative Republican governor of California, defeated Carter in the November 1980 Presidential election. That began an eight-year shift of national politics further to the right than we had seen in half a century. One of Reagan's first actions was breaking a strike of the Air Traffic Controllers Organization. The union was decertified, signaling an attack on the very concept of labor organizing.

Reagan was opposed to big government as well as anti-union; he opposed any cause that those on the left might view as progressive or beneficial to the common good. We joked at the time that he intended to merge the Anti-Trust

Division of the Department of Justice with the Civil Rights Division to create the Anti-Civil-Rights Division. Within a few years, he threatened to pull all funding from the Corporation for Public Broadcasting, a major factor leading to the financial crisis for my primary journalistic outlet, NPR.

I had always supported labor's right to organize. I put this belief into action in my own work by collaborating with other independent radio reporters and producers in the creation of the Association of Independents in Radio (AIR) and negotiation of better terms with the Corporation for Public Broadcasting for freelance audio producers. Since I also freelanced as a reporter for written news sources such as newspapers, magazines, book publishers, and nascent online media, I organized the first Chicago chapter of the National Writers Union (NWU). I'm proud to say that both organizations still exist to protect the rights of contract writers and audio producers.

As these organizations were launched, I began to contemplate what I called "the original labor movement" – i.e., childbearing. I had not anticipated the complexities of being a married woman working within a singles environment. There was a lot of sexual activity among my colleagues, and I encountered some men who tried to seduce me away from a faithful marriage, especially at moments when it appeared that I was feeling rejected by my spouse. I had begun to feel the biological pull of childbearing, but struggled with the decision, partly because of my desire for independence and partly due to uncertainties I felt about bringing children into a world that, too often, seemed fraught with broken families, cruelty, violence, and fears.

I took several steps to sort out my own desires. When I wrote to my one sister who has no children of her own, she wrote back about grief she felt for her unborn children, having made that choice. I found a therapist to address my deep feelings of loneliness and estrangement from my partner as he worked long hours as a law firm associate. I had a heart-to-heart talk with a woman who was older than me, a member of the Writers Union, and the mother of twin teenaged daughters. We were in her living room working on a union event when both girls walked down the stairs from their bedroom. She thrust her arms forward toward them, smiled broadly and said, "How can you not want that joy?"

The combination of my sister's grief, input from my therapist who had young children, and my writer friend's joy in her daughters made it clear to me – I wanted children of my own. Then, considering the advances of men other than my spouse, I weighed the question: who do I really want as the father of my children? However much estranged I felt from my husband at that moment, the answer was obvious to me. I wanted desperately to give the gift of fatherhood to Barry, because I was certain he would flourish as a dad and help me create the home I envisioned for my children.

After Barry had been earning a higher salary at the law firm, I urged him to join me in a home-buying search. We set our sights on a cute two-bedroom brick bungalow just north of Chicago in an Evanston, Illinois neighborhood known as "milkman's row," since it was where that class of workers had lived during the era of milk delivery. As soon as we moved in, my heart was set on making the second bedroom a nursery.

By May 1985, Barry and I had been trying to get pregnant for about nine months. It was not so clear that he, like many of us, was truly ready for this major change in our lives. I discussed that with my therapist, and I saw my gynecologist to ask if we should explore our respective fertility. As it turned out, I was already pregnant! Certain that this was what I wanted, I began to reassess my career and life priorities. By the time our first child was born in early 1986, Barry and I embraced our new roles as parents. Lofty ideals about revolution, rights, and organizing power gave way to the joys and challenges of raising children as a working mother. Selections from those years about our young, growing children can be found in this section.

Mothers love to share their childbirth tales, but not everyone wants to hear them. Suffice it to say that my firstborn was a son, born two weeks late in a fully natural birth with no drugs after about 20 hours of labor. We chose the name Nathan, which means gift of God in Hebrew, because we really felt that this baby was a miraculous treasure.

When Nathan was born, Barry had been working for several years as an associate in a private law firm that was notoriously family-**Un**friendly. Affairs between staff members there abounded and paternity leave for male associates was a pipe dream. The partners with whom Barry worked ridiculed him for taking off a couple days beyond the day of birth. After promising me he would be home for two weeks, he was pressured to go back to the office on the Monday after the Wednesday on which our son was born.

When I learned of this, my post-partum hormones raged and I kicked a hole in the kitchen wall. To his credit, Barry remained very calm and simply said, "I wish you hadn't done that." Some time later, he repaired and repainted the wall. However, I realized there would be no one to offer me physical relief from the demands of birth recovery and caring for a screaming babe with colic. The following week, I had some post-partum bleeding and I had to rest whenever possible to fully heal.

My children were born before the age of Google internet searches. Moms relied on advice from family and friends for parenting tips beyond those of Dr. Spock's book or their pediatrician. Nathan was a colicky baby who ate voraciously but screamed in pain while he digested my breast milk. My friend Bonne had a colicky baby girl a few months earlier and I remain forever in her debt for recommending that I rush out immediately and buy a baby swing. I did what she suggested, and the mechanical swing calmed Nathan immensely, providing both me and my baby with some greatly needed respite. I learned to quickly accept that childbirth and newborn care create new limits on a woman's physical endurance.

After several weeks of searching, I found a young woman to work in our home as our nanny while I returned to a three-day per week, six-hour per day consulting schedule as a reporter/producer of stories for a children's radio program. This enabled me to continue nursing for several months. I had set up a workspace and tape-editing studio in the basement, making it feasible to use a manual pump to supply breast milk to the nanny upstairs. But this did not spare me from the emotional roller coaster of hearing my infant cry when he was hungry, at which point my milk would "let down."

They say you should never have regrets, never second guess the past. But I will always regret leaving my baby for a brief weekend to fly to a writers' union conference in New York City when he was just shy of four months old. As a result, my breastfeeding ended before I intended, and some physical closeness with my infant came to an end. But a benefit was that Barry bonded with his baby son in a new and welcome way.

My life settled into an enjoyable rhythm of part-time work and part-time mothering. I fondly recall the fun of exercising with other moms and our babies, then working out at home while six-month-old Nathan joined me in his "Jolly Jumper" to the music of Talking Heads. I spent days setting up a foam wall around our front sunroom to give this physically precocious baby a safe space for crawling and cruising. By nine months he was walking and running, and I've had trouble keeping up with him ever since.

I lost my pregnancy weight and got back into shape, and Barry and I found a new intimacy as parents. Unfortunately, our calm was harshly disrupted in August 1986, when Nathan's six-month-old nighttime cries awakened us to a masked home intruder. (See a full retrospective story of this experience among the Decade V pieces). About a year later, Barry's firm was swallowed up in a merger, and he sought and accepted a job as an Associate District Attorney with the Manhattan District Attorney Robert Morgenthau.

So, in the summer of 1987, we made a major move back east, sold the first home we owned in Evanston, Illinois and bought a co-op apartment in the up-and-coming Park Slope neighborhood of Brooklyn, New York. We moved from our 1200-sqare-foot bungalow with a full attic, basement, back yard, and detached garage to an 850-square-foot cooperative apartment with on-street parking, no laundry, a small area of basement storage, and a tiny back yard you accessed by crawling through the master bedroom window – all at a price that exceeded the purchase price of our former home by more than $50,000.

After we moved, the entire front room of our railroad flat was crammed to the ceiling with boxes that I slowly unpacked while Barry endured an intense period of prosecutorial training, involving long hours and an unpredictable subway commute. It was a tough transition with a nearly two-year-old toddler, but eventually we settled into the vibrancy of the "Slope" with its charming multi-ethnic environment of shops, restaurants, food co-op, and best of all, the natural beauty, rolling hills, and outdoor escape of Prospect Park, just one block away. There were many other young families in Park Slope, giving Nathan plenty of contact with children his age and providing us with connections to parents whose company we enjoyed. In addition to families whom we met in our neighborhood, we socialized with Barry's colleagues from the Manhattan DA's office, most of whom also had young children.

I found a wonderful neighborhood childcare center called Great Expectations owned and operated by an energetic Black woman named Lelia, with several bright, warm moms as staff. Nathan loved his time there, and I was able to return to freelance radio work for NPR out of their NYC bureau. Nathan enjoyed playing ball in our long hallway, running ahead of us down the sidewalk, riding his tricycle, jumping through the sprinklers at the park in the hot summer sun, and going out for breakfast early Saturday or Sunday with his dad to give mom a chance to sleep in.

Barry's public servant salary and my freelance reporter's income proved insufficient to meet the high costs of living in NYC that included childcare expenses. After several months of continuing my freelance reporting from NPR's New York City Bureau, I was offered a job filling in for that bureau's business reporter who was going on maternity leave. When it became clear that I had to be on call, reporting around the clock as necessary during the market crash of late 1987, I said, "No, thanks. I want to have time with my son." Soon thereafter, I was offered a job at The Brooklyn Historical Society as its Public Relations Director, a job with consistent 9-to-5 hours.

The Society was a short subway ride from the Slope to Brooklyn Heights, in a beautiful nineteenth century landmark building. The job involved a lot of creative spark, working with librarians, curators, graphic designers, and more. The content focus was Brooklyn's history as an amalgam of an incredibly diverse set of communities and an icon of popular culture, featuring the Dodgers, the Honeymooners TV characters, the Navy Yard, and the many ethnic festivals that continue to grace the streets of Brooklyn today. The vision of its Director David Kahn turned the Society into a twenty-first-century museum that celebrates diversity, while respecting its nineteenth-century legacy as a source of genealogical research for white families who had settled in Brooklyn much earlier.

By late 1988, I was thrilled to be pregnant again. The day that this was confirmed at the doctor's office, I returned to work and was called into my boss's office. He offered me a new role and a promotion that would require a more demanding schedule. The conflicted look on my face must have betrayed my condition. I told him I needed to discuss it with my husband and would get back to him the next day. I went right to his office when I got in the next morning and explained that I had just learned I was pregnant. After a day spent trying to figure out if he could afford to pay me enough to cover childcare for both a pre-school child and an infant, he made it clear this was not going to work. I told him I would work through the end of July 1989 and assisted with recruiting my successor.

I was thrilled to learn that I would give birth to a baby girl. We agreed to name her after two of my favorite elders – my great Aunty Jo (Josephine), with whom I had spent several weeks during my summers as a young child, and Barry's maternal grandmother, Anna, who had warmly welcomed me into the Ginsberg/Rosenfeld families regardless of my lack of Jewishness. "Come in my friend," Anna said, "I teach you some Jewish."

Joanna's birth was far quicker and easier than her older brother's. In fact, she was nearly born in the hospital elevator on the way to the maternity ward. As a baby, her temperament was calm and quiet. While her brother, when he awoke, stood up in his crib and yelled, "Momma, momma!" Joanna lay quietly looking around her and singing softly to herself. As with Nathan, I nursed

Joanna for the first several months, without the benefit of today's electric breast pumps. For working moms who wanted to nurse their infants, the only solution was a manual pump that simply did not yield the milk supply my babies needed. I had to supplement with formula, and gradually my milk supply dwindled, leading me to wean both babes earlier than I had desired. But I appreciated my own recovered energy when breastfeeding ended.

One of the most positive revolutions since the 1980s has been the tools, policies, and practices available to many working mothers and fathers. Better pre-natal care, greater attention to teaching breastfeeding tips, online forums for sharing advice, longer parental leave for both moms and dads, whether caring for their own birth children or adopted children – all of these have been valuable additions to the child-rearing village. And most recently, the SARS-COV2 pandemic spurred technologies and employer permission that have enabled parents to work from home. While this created an enormous challenge for working parents with children of school age, it eased the burden for parents of younger babies.

I am sure that many women, men, and nonbinary adults can have extremely fulfilling, meaningful, and joyful lives without having children of their own – whether biological or adopted. But I am just as certain, perhaps more so, that my children have brought the greatest joy and meaning into my life. This does not denigrate my accomplishments or the happiness I've found in other areas of my life, nor does it reflect in any way upon the lives of others, with or without children.

* * *

During the weekend of July 4, 1989, we had arisen with the sun and our three-year-old son. I was eight months pregnant, due in mid-August. We had breakfast, and packed our car to the gills, planning to drive eight hours north to Bethlehem, New Hampshire, where my husband's parents had a small vacation home. We were still at our Park Slope apartment for our final bathroom break and last-minute packing.

At about seven a.m., the telephone (land lines only at that time) rang. The sound of my brother-in-law's voice at that hour told me immediately that something was very wrong. "Your mother has had a stroke. Joan is on the way to the hospital with her now. I think you need to meet her there."

I took down the information about the hospital and arranged to call from a pay phone on our way north to get an update on my mother's condition and how serious the stroke was. We agreed that we would go north until we had to make the decision – do we turn west to head to Syracuse, NY, or northeast toward New Hampshire. When I called my sister at the hospital, we decided to go west to meet her there. My mother was in ICU, but they allowed me to see her.

Her eyes were closed when I leaned down to say, "I love you, Mom." She was able to say, "I love you all." I cried, unable to be certain that she would make it through that night. We stayed in Syracuse, and I was happy to see the next morning that she had made a significant recovery, able to sit up, speak, and eat. We decided to continue on our vacation trip to New Hampshire.

But a couple weeks later, serious medical errors were made by a medical resident who had assumed responsibility for her case when the lead doctor went on vacation. Instead of ceasing all blood thinners as the family insisted, the resident kept her on a new blood thinner and added aspirin, which also has blood-thinning properties. Within days, she had another hemorrhagic stroke that left her entire right side paralyzed and her speaking ability severely damaged. I was too late in my pregnancy to travel back to the hospital to see her.

At that time, my father was deep into a case of Alzheimer's Disease. How deeply, my siblings and I learned when my mother became incapacitated, which left my father, in later stages of dementia, like a toddler with no full-time caregiver. I am grateful I had five siblings who were able to carry the burden of our parents' decline while I carried my baby to her birth in mid-August. The next time I saw my parents, about six weeks after our daughter was born, they were both in a skilled nursing home.

The first time I visited my now-disabled parents at the Birchwood Health Center in Liverpool, New York, it was clear that my father was distraught and unable to understand how he had landed there. My mother seemed to accept her fate, but it was hard to tell since her entire right side was paralyzed and she had severe aphasia, unable to bring thoughts and words from her brain to her mouth. When I said goodbye to my mother, I walked toward the front entrance with my father. As we got to the lobby, my newborn baby girl started to cry, and my three-old son started whining and tugging on my leg. Then my father began to cry, and I thought I would melt into a puddle of horror and distress. My husband said, "Oh my God," and tried to soothe our little boy.

A social worker came out to the lobby from the front office, saw what was happening, and rushed over to take my father's arm. She said, "You can go, your dad will be fine. We'll take good care of him." My husband picked up our son and tugged me toward the door as the nursing home staff walked my dad back to his room. When we got the kids into their car seats and got on our way, I broke down crying.

I include poems from the period prior to and following this health crisis.

Whatever anyone's thoughts, beliefs, or feelings about revolutionary fervor, they often pale in comparison to the challenges of everyday family existence and the major passages in a lifetime.

PIECES WRITTEN BETWEEN 1980 - 1989

1980

Magenta and black
Are back in fashion
Blood and death
Stiletto heels on tight-laced boots
Dressed to kill.

Published February 1980 by *The Chicago Tribune*

Below is the entire letter sent to the newspaper. The section that was published is bolded.

In response to Michael Novak's column of February 21, "Woman as soldier: Reality defied"

There are so many false assumptions in Novak's column on Women and the Draft that I hardly know where to begin.

The tradition of feminism in the U.S. does not lead to women in combat boots. The women's movement has always strived for two essentials: respect for all human beings as individuals, and freedom of choice for women as well as men.

The draft is no choice – for men or women. War is the ultimate "masculine" solution. Feminism demands equal consideration for tradition "feminine" solutions: cooperation, not competition; understanding, not aggression; peace-making, not war-making.

I see absolutely no victory in women going into the military for the protection of a masculine, competitive, capitalist, and ultimately destructive system.

I am NOT saying that an individual or a nation never needs to defend itself. I am NOT saying that women should never take up arms. I AM saying that American women should not take up arms to protect an economic system that has unjustly exploited men, women, children, the family and all the nations of the world.

I would fight for true democracy. I would fight for self-determination. I would fight for freedom. (What do you think women have been doing in the women's movement, anyway?)

I would not fight for multi-national corporations and centralized world bankers' power. I would not fight for a wasteful, overly-consumptive society in a world where millions die of want. I would not fight for nuclear proliferation. I would not fight for a world economic system that has pitted nation against nation, race against race, man against woman, parent against child. I will not fight a war that no one will really win.

Give women something to believe it. Give us a good future for our sons and daughters. We will fight to the death for that.

Linda M. Wagner

On Being American
1980

Don't put that
Finger, strong-arm, vice-grip
Pressure on me.

Don't put that
Guilt, repression, purist trip
On me.

I am an American
What I please
Is what I get
And you're no better that
Yourself.

You lay your trip-trap
On my head
An ideology, you say,
But it's just your ego
Shouting mine down,
Not some higher truth
Or revealed word
It's just your Nazi ego
Self, your mouth
Opened wider than mine.

I am an American,
A No-man's land citizen
A free-for-all
For a price
The price
Is playing the price's game

I live in a nation
Conceived in liberty
A rebel's cause that
Sanctions rebel causes
That molds me into
Uniqueness
That teaches me
I have to push for
What I want and that's OK –
Step on the toes
Of those who haven't learned the rules 'til
They do and make your match.

I am an American
I am what I buy
My spending
Proclaims my identity
Financial priorities
Determine my friends,
My work, my class

I am an American
A stereotype
If Black
I buy a Cadillac
If blue collar
I buy American
If a doctor
I buy economy
If a playboy
I buy a sports car.

We are all selves
Screaming, tantrum-throwing
Children
We want our way
We want our way

I am an American
I can't escape
The bondage of
My Self.

The Future of the Past in American Journalism

1980 Unpublished Essay

After the Soviet invasion of Afghanistan, U.S. Secretary of Defense Harold Brown visited China. He was there to develop the potential for military cooperation between the two vast nations. One Chinese official reacted to his suggestions by saying, "You Americans are charming. You forget the past so quickly."

During the ongoing Iranian revolution, Iranian criticisms of the American press mounted to the point that nearly all American journalists were expelled from the country for a period of time. One of the major contentions that Iranian officials made during the mounting tensions was that the media in the United States had a short memory, in this case, about the Shah's regime and the American government's support of that regime. Despite their own apparent lack of freedom of the press, and their efforts to manipulate the Western world's media, the Iranian criticism contains an important element of truth.

When you open the daily newspaper or watch TV newscasts, you are swept into a world of the present at the edge of the future. Reports of what has just happened and anticipation of what will come next are the primary fare of American reporting. Conspicuously absent is what has gone before.

There are exceptions, of course. There are the two outside columns of *The Wall Street Journal*'s front page, the *Christian Science Monitor*, some articles in *The New York Times*, National Public Radio's *All Things Considered* news program, and the all-too-infrequent documentary-style series in newspapers or on TV.

But the overwhelming bulk of information presented to the American public offers little or no sense of history. All the consequences of this two-dimensionality (the two dimensions being present and future) are difficult to determine. However, it seems clear that it limits American understanding of many other nations whose rich sense of history is offended by American ignorance. It limits our understanding of ourselves as well.

It might be said that this blindness to the past has shaped American character and even led to its past successes. It is a character molded by a "free enterprise" mentality that forges ahead aggressively, often failing to consider not only the past but the future too. For example, who had the foresight to plan for the waste products of the huge chemical and nuclear industries? Who used hindsight in order to glean a lesson from the pollution problems created by earlier sources of energy like coal?

"Historical reporting," it might be said, "is analysis, and therefore has no place in the reporting of today's events. Leave it to the individual reader or viewer to know history."

It cannot be denied that the reporting of the past is a dangerous enterprise. Even in reporting the present, the reporter's perspective plays a role in his or her selection of what is fact and what is not. While the press is busy reporting the moment, it has ideological biases to which we are often blind because they are so close to us.

For example, whether we report that American hostages are being held by "students," "militants," "Iranians," or simply "captors" tells us more about our view of who those captors are than about the captors. How many of the reports we've read or seen have told us about the political and historical development of those captors in a way that would shed light on why they are doing what they are doing?

Such an ideological bias raises many questions. Is the press to be concerned that the American public understands what is happening, or simply that they know what the moment holds? Is the American press supposed to report human news? Or do its boundaries stop at American or Western news? Should American journalists simply accept and adopt the American character mentioned above, aggressively forging ahead in the reporting of the events of the moment?

The ideological biases often present in news reports may, in large part, be a result of reporters' ignorance of history of the U.S. and the world. But in today's world of global economy, shifts in world power, and international communication, ignorance and ignoring of history on the part of American journalists cannot be excused.

Knowledge of history, presentation of historical facts, and presentation of the disputes over historical facts when there are such disputes, are responsibilities of journalists. They require unusually high standards of source checking and balanced reporting.

The American press should grasp these responsibilities in the area of international affairs as well as it grasped them in the reporting of Chappaquiddick. It should use history as a tool to further public understanding of local, national, and international events and issues. When it ignores the past, which is the context of the present, it leads the public ignorantly through the present into what, I fear, is a very dark future.

Have Faith

May 6, 1980

Once a friend said to me, "If you started a new religion, I'd belong to it." She was a secular feminist Jew and I had been raised Roman Catholic. Her comment may have been a tremendous compliment. But it also demonstrated that many of us crave a new "religion."

So many of the values in our established religions no longer apply easily to the conflicts in our lives. It's important to remember - God, nature, and the universe haven't changed their essence since those religions were founded. But the world has evolved. Religions are tied to historical periods and tied to human experience. But God, nature, and the universe, as basic principles, remain. And frankly, they could all get along just as well without us.

It's important to remember that. Scientists tell us the human species did not always exist. Even our religions tell us so. If we have imagined a universe without the human being, is it so hard to imagine the human species might again disappear?

Time has not eroded the wisdom of the saying, "Necessity is the mother of invention." Now, the necessity is that we cooperate and understand each other. What will we invent to do that? The possibilities are endless. Bringing women into full equality is one way of reaching our goals. Why? Because for untold centuries, women have carried on traditions and values of cooperation, compassion, understanding. Throughout human history, woman has been delegated the role of keeping the family intact.

But the family has grown. People of different skin colors and cultures have embraced each other and mingled throughout the centuries. Women have a new, much larger family in their care. And we must do it as passionately as we care for our very own individual child.

The entire human family is in jeopardy. We face real threats of self-extinction. Women know this in our bones. Women who rave so emotionally against abortion on demand know this. They know when society encourages abortion, society is in jeopardy. But those anti-abortion advocates do not identify the correct source of the danger. They lash out at symptoms because they fear the message the symptoms represent.

Many of us who struggle for the right to abortion on demand fear the underlying danger itself. For when society does not nurture the mother, how can she nurture the child?

Despair creeps in. Shouldn't we simply retreat to our homes? Won't that solve this crisis? No, because the crisis is IN our homes. The crisis permeates our very existence. Where can we turn?

Jesus gave us the message: Love your neighbor. We need a variation on that theme today. I say: Believe in yourself, then believe in your neighbor. Believe in each other.

The prophets have always been men. Perhaps God has ordained in heaven an equal rights amendment for women. Perhaps the new message bearers are women.

But who is listening?

On Whether the Death Penalty is Ever Warranted

1980

Would you tell me to feel sorry
For a grown man who has choked
The life out of 33 boys?
Gacy, you have inexcusable nerve
And an ego so large it takes
Four personalities to distribute it.
O mutilators of little animals
And unsure young children
O killers who know better
Than to do what they do
O society who pretends
Not to see
O world that will not acknowledge
The searching sorrow in the eyes,
You are one and the same....
Stop this madness,
And teach a human to be human
To make contact
To touch souls
To be honest, above all
To be honest.

Wired 1980

Plug your data bank
Into my program
We'll lay down
Some heavy calculations
My input and your output
My software and your hardware
Just speak my computer language baby

Ruminations
1980 – 1983

July 1980 Conversation with a Friend on Current Politics

"I can't get worried about these elections anymore," she said. "They seem so removed from my life."

I replied, "You may think they're removed now. But if Reagan is elected, you'll feel differently within about a year."

"You're being paranoid. How much difference can he really make?"

"It's not him that makes the difference. It's the fact that there are enough people who are foolish enough to elect him." "Look. Those people will vote for him no matter who I vote for. Voting for Carter just to ensure Reagan doesn't get elected is just the same old, same old."

"What about Anderson, then?"

"I don't want John Anderson. I don't believe in him any more than Carter. The only one who's saying things that I think are important is Barry Commoner."

"Who?"

"See? Most people don't even know he's running. The media doesn't even bother covering it. He's too small for them."

September 4, 1980

I feel sad about the suffering of others that I can't see how to alleviate.

I saw Abbie Hoffman on TV. Bob Dylan is now a Jesus freak, Rubin is on Wall Street, Jane Fonda is in the movies. They have been with us in the coalitions and the revolution. We remain as the "revolution" and will reap the consequences.

November 1980 Nightmares to the Tune of Living in a Material World

The USA has elected Ronald Reagan president. I fear the dissolution of the meaning of nuclear – the pro nuke family and pro nuke power versus cellular health and reconstruction. My star is fading and before long will die. I can only shine with what energy I have remaining and hope the light reaches someone who will use it wisely. I see the scenes of destruction vividly – foresight engraved on my retina. For being myself, I will be in pain. Not the first time, of course, but perhaps the last. A steady drift towards the ungluing of centripetal forces. The potential for fascism is overwhelming. I am numb. Political paralysis has struck.

November 1981

The New York Times has an article about Nicaragua and Alexander Haig yesterday. Even though I've finished my refugee story about Salvadorans and planned to work on a Saudi business story, my dreams revolved around the girls and priests in Nicaragua, their push to get to freedom, the burning houses, and U.S. military dollars. I had forgotten, so long past Vietnam, the feeling of shame in my country. How it gently, quietly, slowly began creeping back when Ronald Reagan said, "I don't want war, but if I did, you're where I'd start." How dare I complain about my choices when in countries next door to mine, the corpses of the young are piled high because they seek the very things I possess?

I chose to come to Chicago, but two teenaged sisters south of our border were forced to escape the threat of death.

December 2, 1981

The worst thing about the trends in my life now is the move away from the outer reaches of creativity and toward political action and organization around bread-and-butter issues for writers. I feel it's essential to my survival, on the one hand, and a good omen for my future. But I need the creative time back in stronger force.

Feminism has been a synthesizer for me, but I've come to feel lost about my strategies, my means versus ends. I feel caught up with confronting the world of male-dominated creativity in a very face-to-face way. I have had to sidestep the nurturance of separatism of women from men. I no longer feel part of a whole. I envy the work of women who take a woman's theme and stick with it. But my own life is multifarious – family, friends, political allies, and work colleagues. I must confront these realities within the USA, President, Ronald Reagan.

Feminists – too many – seem to be hiding in a world of illusion. I understand the need to build our own world apart, but I live in this patriarchal although changing system each day. I find that the creative world, dominated by male insensitivity, is one of the final bastions. I want to attack it. But am I then playing at their own game?

Men will not forgive an angry woman easily. They say, OK, you try to do it on your own. You try to face what I, as a man, must face. That's not pretty either, it's true.

I want to read, hear, see, touch the thoughts of women. But instead, I read male authors. I am criticized by too many peers for hiding my own head from my work. I want to do radio stories, write articles, poetry, fiction, write, write, write. But there are these endless details in which I lose myself. The distractions, the wasted emotional energy, the involvement with other people that keeps me from myself, from my own rhythms.

I feel I've put in my time for organizing and being political, and I want to be alone now. But I know I must continue to synthesize. I must listen to the call of my soul, or my work will go nowhere at all.

January 24, 1982

Values, the bane of my existence. I rise and push myself through the day like a moray eel through ocean water, yet with moral decision-making that such an animal never weighs. Is my development beyond instinct a tool for survival and growth or a hindrance?

Lately, being on the spot for the values I've chosen, accepted, embraced, I need to clarify them myself. I used to say, "I think I'm a socialist." Yet when I heard Bahai beliefs described, I nearly said, "I think I'm a Bahai." The community I see, however, is illusory, transient. Community occurs due to a confluence of de facto factors or an effort of organizing. I state most clearly that I am a feminist. But can I define that further?

So, I am now reluctant to attach any "ism" label to myself, although others would do so. I am most clearly a feminist because I have joined feminist organizations and even organized some. While I adhere to certain "socialist" principles, I have never joined such a group. I am not entirely convinced of the effectiveness of socialist – at least not American socialist – parties or platforms. The Soviet social and economic systems have been disastrous. China and Cuba accomplished much for the bases of their populations. But none of these systems are at the end of progress. The American system held more promise, but perhaps that was because the ideology of American revolution was housed in an undeveloped land with incomparable resources. And because its development relied on the destruction of indigenous peoples and the enslavement of others.

I still think there's a need to "nationalize" basic industries, but national state ownership is not, I think, the real solution. The public-private partnership concept is good at its core, but it's too little too late as it now exists. I think the first step is to make people realize the extent of state/corporate connection that already exists. The American public has no clear idea of the real structure of economic power. In fact, the society is pluralistic, the economy is diversified.

But we're witnessing a strong minority pushing hard for a more monolithic center, and it's impossible to achieve that while growing the economy for all of us. The real task is to make pluralism and diversity work together. Fighting that is suicide.

So, my politics are pragmatic. A working system is what I want to see. An end to racial discrimination is desirable because racism prevents positive resources from entering and enriching the society as a whole. Ditto with sexism and homophobia.

All this religious revival is, to me, a mish mash. Religion is really about the relationship of an individual human being to the Totality/yin-yang/Godhead/unifying force. The understanding of this relationship is personal, i.e. my relationship to the Universe. How can it be codified? True prayer and thanks are songs from the heart. To gather in church is to seek a community of shared values with other people, not to seek God. To seek the spiritual, the mystical, requires solitude. Truths are revealed personally, individually. Shared experiences reinforce security, not necessarily truth.

There is a human need to gather. But with what group? I believe in the gathering of all groups. I haven't seen it anywhere yet, although the Bahai faith is close. Even there, the activity does not gel, at least not for me.

Early 1982

What is so bad about self-love in women? What is so wrong with looking in the mirror and saying, "I like you (me)?"

All this concern about narcissism and the "me decade" comes from men whose women are watching out for themselves for a change. Men have been in the "me decade" for centuries. But let women show some concern about their own well-being and there are screams and whimpers that western civilization is falling apart.

To be concerned about yourself, your own sanity, health, and welfare – this is the most sensible thing a woman can do. We should not feel guilt at our positive self-image that we have struggled so hard to build. We earned our narcissism. We fought and worked hard for the right to say, "this time, me first."

I am not condoning selfishness nor deriding the traditionally female virtues of compassion, sacrifice, and altruism. I am just saying it is time to change traditions. It is time for men to nurture, give in, compromise.

The 1979 film Kramer versus Kramer forces that point. And in the end, the woman must NOT have everything. None of us, men or women, should want or have everything. But men must realize the trade-offs from them that are necessary. They must experience the rewards of sacrifice.

We don't need women who become just like men. And we don't need men who become just like women.

We need human beings who just become human.

1982

It is not that you ignored an underpinning of post-Vietnam America, but that you did not place it in contextual focus. It was not simply that America was defeated by Vietnam, but that West was defeated by East. Our two countries were simply the vehicles, the stage for the playing of centuries-old tensions between two very different world views, not unlike Gandhi's struggle with the British in India.

The East's victory has had an enormous impact on American culture upon which your articles barely touched. In just the city of Chicago, there are now dozens of Oriental martial arts schools. Yoga, Tai Chi, and other Asian classes are offered regularly for relaxation and toning at YMCAs across the USA. Thousands of Toyotas, Datsuns, and Hondas grace our highways; Japanese management is in vogue; prints of Chinese and Japanese brush paintings abound on walls in the homes of American Blacks, Jews, white Anglo-Saxons, Irish, Italians, and more. Yuppies eat regularly at Thai restaurants while Japanese designer dresses are in fashion. If you were born after 1970, all of this would seem to be a given of American life. But the influence of Asian culture was rarely felt outside the Chinatowns of California and New York City prior to the U.S. defeat by Vietnam.

In Vietnam, the USA discovered it had much to learn, not only from our closer antiquities of Greece, Rome, and the grandiose British Empire. But from the Han Dynasty, Samurai, Buddhism, Tao, and Hindu thought. We discovered that the Eastern *"weltanschauung"* was another way for the human mind to perceive reality. The shock of Vietnam was that of the American mind, then quintessentially Western, coming face-to-face with its mirror opposite. The wild, unbridled Texas cowboy with his patent disregard for nature and his short memory fought a war against a people who had developed a timeless tradition of discipline, patience, and efficiency tempered by deep, biting, historical remembrance.

It is claimed that Nietzsche said, "Be careful who you choose as your enemy because that's who you become most like." It is especially true when you march blindly and headstrong into battle and lose. This is one lesson the USA is still learning.

Embedded Love Lost

What did you share that now,
Your voice catches on her name
And chokes, unable to continue?
And where is that pain stored?
In no leg or arm or bloody innards
Where it's easy to point out
The pain is etched in your every movement
Every tremor of your voice
Every glimmer in your eyes
Unable now to say
The things you said to her
Not hearing her response
Her unspoken understandings
Longing for the aura of her presence in the room
The vibration of her energy
Now that she is gone.

Someone I Admire – May 1981

She is someone I admire
Far away from home
Standing up for things that she believes.

She is strong and lean, yet warm
And smiles even when it's hard
To feel any joy.

Words don't stick in her throat.
Dishes never fall from her hands
I let tears flow only for the wounds of others.

She knows when she's right and stands firm
But will always admit when she's wrong
And a harmful lie never passes her lips.

She can sense when her oddities
Make others squirm
And works to put them aside to get across.

But when art and craft serve her purpose
She employs those talents
And creates a work of genius.

She is citizen of no one country
Patron of no single cause
She embraces the human in failure and achievement.

Of Children, At Age 29

Your breeze-blown faces
Roll in my sky mind
Niece, nephew, child born
Of friends and strangers.

I've reached that woman's age
Each infant throws
Whispered echoes
Of some biological fate.

To my queries, blood sisters and dear friends –
They have sons and daughters in their lives –
Say yes
It's hard, but irreplaceable.
They're the new technique
A painter learns, to create
Desired effect on canvas
They're the catalyst
In a reaction chain, moving
Mom and dad to some new synthesis
Simply they
Are life proceeding
From the carnal.

When it's done, human cloud
Mingled with human flesh
And arriving at our front door
The questioning goes out the back
Just joy or regret
Remains, embodied.

An acorn never asks to live its own life
Without rooting
Why do I?
I am not just a seed-containing shell
I am still
The seed still
The blossom still
The fruit.

To Mom and Dad, To Life

February 1982

Won't you stretch your arms high
To meet the remaining years with delight?
You must see the first edition of
The book I've not yet written
You must see the painted picture
Of our parting years
When our souls were torn by love

You thought I hid behind poetry
Not seeing or hearing within me
The echoes of your own forgotten dreams

But I've known you too long myself
Seen dad's hand artfully sketch
Column ads of Mohegan's special sales
And mom's quizzical eyes daring to fathom
The mysteries of a flower
Dad blocked from the engineer's drafting quarters
Mom shut out from biologists' laboratories
You've engineered, concocted
A grand family design
Using all the talents
Of science, art, and nature
And the tough commitment
Of tender love

We are your offspring
Walking symbols of your aspiration
That was choked by a world
Beyond your control
Where circumstance stopped
Your youthful exploration

With our "lofty" degrees
We are not scissors
To cut you off from the future
But bridges back to those hopes
You thought you'd lost in 1931.

1982
The Lost Art of Ideation

Ideas are cheap these days. I'm not so old, yet I remember a time when ideas were sculpted and crafted like a wooden statue of the one you love. You started with a crude, rough hunk of solid thought. You checked over it carefully to make there were no knotholes, no imperfections in the grain. Then, satisfied that the basic stuff could withstand the hacking and chipping of argument, you played your own devil's advocate. Your self-critique was your carving knife. Each counterpoint to your thesis produced a curve or a niche that gave shape to the idea and eliminated the dead wood of excess.

Once your beloved statue took form, you refined it with the sandpaper of research and polished it with the finish of certainty. Your thought, carved and based on a solid foundation, was then draped with a cloak of elegant language, ready to be revealed. This presentation of the idea is itself an art, but the message inhering in the form is evidence of a richer art – the creation of ideas.

Today, too many ideas are cranked out and packaged like deodorant or cereal. The craft of ideation has given way to automated thoughts, made to conveniently fit into ideologies like cogs in machinery. The care is gone, and so goes the art.

When Radical Change Is Necessary

Emotional difficulties burden all of us. The form varies and some people do not appear to share in this human infirmity. It's likely that those folks have not yet gone through experiences that challenge their faith in their belief system. They can aggravate people who are in the midst of crisis. Their calm demeanor, smile, relaxed attitudes about everything that comes their way – it may make you want to vomit. They seem so sickishly sweet, so boringly self-assured.

But to those in the thick of it, even those who have been through their own crises and come out on the other side are a source of anxiety and jealousy. They appear to have it all together. For the person in trauma, these people can make you feel even more isolated. They are not sweet; they are tough. They do not agree that you cannot make it through your crisis. After all, they made it through theirs.

You may be suffering through the loss of faith in your spouse – perhaps he or she breeched your trust. Your toughened friend may have lost faith in his profession, or even in a political leader. There is common ground in "ground-lessness." That is, neither of you has the ground of belief on which to stand. You are going through an emotional floating. Before, faith had served as the gravity that kept you standing upright on solid soil. Now, despair leaves you intellectually weightless. Your perceptions can no longer be so easily pigeon-holed. With your belief construct gone, there is no longer a box in which to place your perceptions. They float freely, crowding together in a disorganized state.

But they will not remain so. This is where the truly exciting and interesting aspects of change enter the picture. You must begin to form a new construct. It's not an easy task. And during this period, you're in danger of insanity, despair, or falling back into the patterns of your old beliefs that are no longer meaningful but offer an illusion of security. None of these alternatives are desirable. You must choose to rebuild if you are going to survive and be happy.

No Compromise

1982

As though I could somehow lapse into a different rhythm
Than the beat that my heart raps out
You ask me to deny the rush of blood in my veins
The quickened pulse, and flash of fury.

Am I fighting on a battlefield
That's overgrown with daisies
Like an aging captain in exile
Who hasn't heard the news:
The war is over?

Or do we stand at the edge
Of a tidal wave backlash
That washes away the gains
Of those who say trustingly
Principle can be compromised sometimes.

In 1982, I live, a woman
In a nation that withholds
A law that states
Equal rights under the law
Shall not be abridged
On account of sex.
Who can afford the compromise?
Me? You?

Aug. 15, 1982

After two and a half years in the flat landscape in and around Chicago, riding through the mountains of New Hampshire feels like stepping into a worn old shoe. I want to move back to the hills and mountains with maples and fir trees. I want to be where I know the geography and demographics like the back of my hand. There's a layered richness that I feel here, customs I find understandable, smells in the air and a greenness that fill me with awe.

Here the ravings of politicians and soldiers are tossed into the corner of significance, where they belong. A desire to do simple, honest, good work swells. Suspicions fade.

Role Play

My role as a woman
These days
Is as a homemaker
In the world
Trying to blend
Discordant voices
Into harmony
Like mom
With six kids
A husband
And her mother at home
Trying
To keep the family
Together.

Behavior Mod

In the tomb of past sins
Near decaying corpses from unsuccessful missions
I find my voice.
A locked trunk, the darkness, a suicide order
From the president of the soul –
I do not obey, but repeat the message
In my fears and needs.
I see my lover grow weeds in his mind,
I see his air passages choke on vines of
Entanglement with me.
I want to kill their growth but know
I'd have to kill the love to stop it.
I become a fountain of dismalness,
Ugly and insipid.

This is the stranger form
Of self-flagellation taught
By the Catholics, the doubts
Of self-worth
A plant nurtured in poison soil,
The wrath of Catholic education
I shall embark on a new course, though,
Built from the stones of resistance –
Lessons taken from freedom-fighters
Acting out my fantasies
In ways that enable me to survive
I tell twisted stories now,
But I'll find new ways to weave them.

Sometimes the words tumble from my mouth
Light and colorful,
And as they shower and spray, they
Find their place in impressive jungles of sound.
But other times, I must pull them from my throat
Like teeth from the roots
And their tone is barbed and broken,
They fall like pellets.

Or I close my voice box
Lock it shut
Pour myself into pages
Try to disappear from the outside in
Then my skin crawls with maggots of perception
Others see me
Feel discomfort emanate in pain rays
To their hearts.

They want me to laugh, and speak
But I'm frightened as a wild kitten
They want me to play, chase after yarns
Jump over furniture
Roll on the floor,
But I must crouch beneath tables
Afraid of being gunned down.

They grew up healthy,
Backs patted, fur stroked
I had indifferent caretakers
But I can't blame the outside
For my excessive need.

Like a flower petal touched with acid
The Child in me recoils at disfavor
Falters under the weight of a few harsh words
Though the hide has toughened
Some reflex remains.

I must face the moments,
cry,
And start over.

Sept. 6, 1982 in Paris

I am so thoroughly engrossed in this trip that it seems to be stretching into forever. Specifically, it is the pleasant memories that I hope will spread into infinity. Two new French friends, sights and sounds of Paris (even though some fear they live on past glory), the sound of a language rich in context and musical connotation.

**Later September 1982 at end of bicycle and
camping trip through Loire Valley:**

One of the clearest impressions I will take away from France is the air - a softness in the air. And gentle lighting that falls upon white, gray, or beige toned walls of stone, brick, stucco or cement. Spending time with the pretty things - landscapes, gardens, art, wide rivers under blue skies. And a gentle breeze through my hair in the late summer shade. The buildings are steeped in the strong leaves of time and the language with its generous inflection and poetic flow make it clear that this this is France!

It makes me feel that we humans are made for nothing more than to roll with a lover in sunny fields, eat fresh fruit and bread and drink fine wine. Here, you can feel in your bones and gut how art is inspired. France is a place that can put the pieces together.

During another break in the travels:

And yet France, some say, lives on past glories. There is disappointment in Mitterrand; confusion over Chirac; questions about whether the right is truly better; fears of whispered fascism awaiting in American wings; disgust with the totalitarianism of corporate, fast-paced efficiency and short-term profit *uber alles*; prostitution simply accepted; the loss of aesthetic sensibilities and culture.

In Europe, 40 years after WWII, body parts are art. A mime dressed as a robotic mannequin is felt expression. Music abounds in the streets, but Parisians lament the deaths of French jazz greats. Black American artists are celebrated, but brown Arab workers are not. And at Palace de Justice, we watch another dark-skinned young man doomed to poor representation in a criminal court.

We are privileged to sit in on a brief Montmartre conversation between parents and child, but these thick American ears do not understand - mourir, mort, who is dead? What is dead? Like echoes of a wailing man in the night's hollow center on Rue Ravignan, who, what is dead? The sound of flesh and bone smacking against flesh and bone; the Israeli guard in front of El Al with machine gun in hand; the fear of Russians, some say worse than fears of Stalin this time.

The intellectual Parisian is torn between the failures of the left and the promises of the right. Sorrow and pity; this is Europe, the lands from which my people came. On the River Seine stands a copy of the New World's open arms promise, while a West German boy with blue eyes and a trade—even he must have a visa to wander the shores of the USA. Our hosts want to go to the land of Miles Davis and big city neighborhoods. They search their souls to find what "typical French" means these days.

After Long Island, NY shopping mall wastelands, the gentle hues of Paris walls and evening light upon the Tuileries makes me gag at the sight of wasted young Parisians gobbling Big Macs and fries, tossing plastic and paper in the paths of Champs Elysees tourists like me.

Dec. 21, 1982 – On work

I'm finding NPR is a good freelance journalism base for pragmatic reasons, but personal relationships get in the way of hard, smart, steady work. I applied for a production job at WTTW-TV and got interviewed but was rejected. I learned later I was not considered "worldly enough" (which to me means "not rich enough.") But I've had much success these past months - a University of Chicago contract, research for BBC-TV, the Teamsters trial assignment from NPR, Satellite News work. On the more creative front, I have a January prose reading coming up next month.

This Writers Union

She sees the clutter of an industry
Like dirtied socks balled up and tossed
In the center of the living room floor
The mess bothers her
The loose ends
That stick out and trip up
Those who try in good faith
To do their work.

One is not paid at all for his efforts,
Another waits four months for the check
"The magazine just folded," says a voice
At the other end of the phone
Bankruptcy means writers,
Always paid last
Go unpaid today

The Reagan Years - To Barry

It all starts quietly enough
The blanket draped across the torso
The TV on, the sound low
A newspaper tossed beside the couch
The inky newsprint photo headlined
"How you too can be a playboy bunny"

It all starts emptily enough
The resonance of nighttime echoes
Against a bedroom wall
The high-pitched whirr of inner ringing
A hastily put-together dinner
A tossed-together wardrobe.

The rope of anchoring cut loose
In a stormy ocean of ideas,
Faces and dreams
Trailing off to undefined values,
Unfocused goals
A President against social change

The seconds dribble by
The chasm grows
East Coast to Midwest
Rebel to stasis
Freedom to a questioned responsibility.

There is the key to someone
Else's door out there.
In dark hallways
The same ones that led to
Secret notebooks

Can bonds so quickly lose
Their meaning?
Outlive their "usefulness"
Or are they just the wrong word?

And where lies the greater threat,
Which road, which railroad track
Which subterranean subway path
Leads to worse than sorrow –
And which points home?

Reflections on Election Day 1983 in Chicago

(In 1983, Chicagoans elected a Black man, Harold Washington, as Mayor.)

Today, the balmy humid air of springtime calms the frazzled nerves of Chicago after a heated election. Yesterday, while voters went to the polls, I took a brisk walk through several precincts in the heavily Black second ward.

On my way from the subway station, a young man approached me to find out who I was, why I was on his turf. Terry, 28 years old, grew up in this neighborhood near broken green glass, shattered and strewn in street-corner lots like the dreams of his friends and neighbors.

"None of the guys what come up with me are still alive. They're all dead," he told me. "They was all drunk on dope or wine when they got killed. But me and my buddy over there, we had politics to keep us busy. Radical politics." Terry had been a member of the Black Panthers in former days, and a follower of Elijah Muhammed. "Today was the first time I voted in my life," he confessed. "My mother convinced me to vote for Harold."

We walked into 3550 South Cottage Grove. The halls were quiet. Terry acted like my bodyguard though we'd met on the streets just moments before, and he'd expressed his disappointment when I answered his question with, "Yes, I'm married. Yes, I'm happily married." He still wanted to protect me while I, a 31-year-old white woman, walked through the ward. "I want to watch how you work here," he said. "I want to see what you do."

What I did was talk to Mr. Williams, the Black Republican poll watcher for Washington's challenger, Bernard Epton. The Reverend Jesse Jackson, a frequently quoted civil rights leader, referred to Epton as "that pathetic bearded creature."

"Yeah," said Mr. Williams, "there will be some votes for Mr. Epton in this precinct."

"Who's going to win?" I asked.

"Mr. Epton, so I hear on the radio. Mr. Epton by 50 thousand."

But two blocks east and two blocks south, the neighborhood looks more like the poverty of the old south transported to a concrete nightmare. "No Epton supporters here," said Vernell, the Democratic election judge. "This is solid hard-core Black folks here. Only Washington votes here." Vernell gestured toward the precinct that Terry and I had just left. "Over there are some middle-class Black folk – Lakefront."

Outside, a young woman with coal black skin could barely look me in the eye, her determination was so fierce that her man would win this time. "You'll find out how we feel when Mr. Washington wins," she told me. Terry walked with me to the bus stop, asking me how I did my work. He told me about confronting the Chicago police in 1968, when he was only 13 years old. He asked for my phone number.

"I want to trade ideas with you," he insisted. But the experienced eyes of a 31-year-old woman caught the desire written on a man's face. The desire for love, for escape that I knew I was unable to provide. "There's gunshots around here every night," Terry said. "It's a jungle. I want to get out of here."

Harold Washington cannot provide Terry with immediate escape from life in the second ward, any more than a young, white, female reporter can. But a Black mayor is hope. Bobby Rush, Terry's favored candidate for Alderman, is hope. Bobby Seals is dead, and so is Martin Luther King. But Terry is still alive. Harold and Bobby Rush are still alive.

Postscript: Harold Washington was elected mayor in April 1983. He died from a heart attack in November 1987. As of August 2023, Bobby Rush, a Black Panther imprisoned for six months in 1972 after carrying a pistol into a police station, is still alive. Rush was elected and served as the U.S. Representative for the

1ˢᵗ *Congressional District of Illinois for 30 years, from January 1993 to January 2023, "with an emphasis on the most vulnerable and the communities that feel left behind," according to his biography. I never learned Terry's last name and I have no idea whether he is still alive or if he was able to get out of the Second Ward.*

1984 - Reagan Likely to Be Re-Elected

The feeling that STOPS me feels like a frown, but it's embedded much deeper than a frown.

Beyond simple fear, it is DESPAIR and DREAD. It's connected to the dark corner of isolation. My despair and dread are over the political climate. The realization that fascism is surrounding me, while I am not able to accept or really see it, because I must live every day. I see it in my work as a reporter, in those things I must cover and remain "objective." When I must tell people that, believe it or not, this is what is happening.

This veneer that "all is well" is frail, thin, easily chipped away.

Revolution in a 1984 Dream

It is only a dream. Our generation is fomenting revolution.
They try to hang my husband and other allies.
They catch me, poison me, shoot me, torture me.
Within the dream, I say that I did it to myself.
I brought it on myself.
It is my punishment for revolutionary fervor.

Values in Conflict and Contradiction

The choice between morality as absolute or situational -

Abortion: I choose to waffle – situational

Fidelity: To be faithful – Love is Trust – an absolute value, once discovered and learned

Capitalism: Not my goal but I see it has some usefulness. Needs to be controlled more than it is.

Communism: Too stilted, too destructive of human expression, but noble in its concept of the common good.

Unionism: Need for a NEW movement

Nationalism: Dysfunctional in today's global world.

His Name, Her Name, and the Law

Published in *The New York Times*, January 8, 1985

To the Editor:

"The Last Name Game: A Balancing Act" (Dec. 17), on women changing their names because of marriage or divorce, did not mention what is perhaps the most fundamental reason why feminists keep their maiden names when marrying. It's the same reason that the New York Court of Appeals just ruled that a husband can be prosecuted for raping his wife.

Historically, in many cultures, a bride assumed the bridegroom's name on their wedding day because she then became the property of her new husband, rather than the property of her father. (Remember, the father "gives the bride away.")

Feminists (and today's American legal system) reject the belief that a human being can be considered property. They also reject the idea that only men can be property owners.

The oversight illustrates that feminism's basic challenges to a pre-existing social order continue to go unrecognized. It's true that keeping the name one has held for a lifetime (even if it's a father's name) can carry psychological benefits to a woman's maintenance of self-identity and career benefits of continued recognition.

But keeping one's name is more than expression of personal style. There is social, legal and moral substance behind this exercise of freedom.

LINDA M. WAGNER

Evanston, Illinois

Worth a Thousand Words

1985

If you were single
It would be corporate mergers
And blond, blue-eyed Karens
Cut from the same tweed cloth
Like paper dolls.

If you were single
It would be dinner
In tasteful restaurants downtown
A new hat each season
Long hours filled with federal express

If you were single
It would be cocktails
Later and later Friday night
A movie, some music
Maybe get laid.

If you were single
It would be no commitment
Saturday morning
Then bump into each other
In the office hallway.

If you were single
It would be so exciting,
Stimulating
Hanging in mid-air
No ending.

If you were single
It would be easy
I would be gone
And, passing you on the street,
I would never want to know you.

Unpublished Letter to Editor, February 3, 1986

To the Editor:

I applaud the widespread coverage of writers and their concerns given by the *NYT* during recent writers' meetings, from the Soviet writers' conference in Moscow to the international PEN conference in New York.

Throughout this coverage, communication barriers between Soviet and American writers have surfaced over and over. At the PEN meeting, they arose due to the simple absence of Soviet authors. William Gass's piece in Sunday's Book Review section on the November meeting between Soviet and American writers in Lithuania shed some light on that absence. His article prompts my letter.

The imprisonment of people for expressing their views or describing the world in their own terms is anathema to us as Americans and writers. The Soviet system or any political system deserves nothing but condemnation for that practice. Yet, as Gass's experience illustrates, we cannot force those Soviet writers who are financially secure and politically free to write due to their Soviet form of "Union membership" to acknowledge this failure of Soviet politics and culture.

We can remind them, of course, and perhaps we'll eventually see some impact. But real change in the Soviet Union must come from those in the "internal" situation with which we're always accused of "meddling." There is, in fact, some reason for hope in the courage of writer/leaders like Yevtushenko.

What is left for us to do as American writers to improve the lot of writers everywhere? There is work to be done at home. Imprisonment does not come to the American writer via "union," work camps, cells, or Siberian winters. Here the writer is kept in tow by economics, not politics. Our political system of democracy, with its guarantees of free expression, holds only promise for writers. (Sadly, non-U.S. citizens seem to be notable exceptions here.)

But our economic system – an increasingly unbridled capitalism of multinational conglomerates that control, among many other industries, the publishing world – does hold a symbolic lock and key for the writer. It's composed of the drive for mass market book sales, high profits, the move toward "information" as commodity rather than knowledge as value, and a growing tendency to hire inexperienced youngsters as editors because they can be paid poorly.

I am not trying to compare the Soviet prison with the American system of "free enterprise." I am saying that it's up to the Soviets to fix what's wrong with their political system. It's up to us to fix what's wrong with our economic system as it affects writers.

American writers shy away from this responsibility, despite the desperate effect the economics of publishing often has on our morale, our ability to support ourselves financially, and worst of all, our vision as writers. The most obscene thing about our system is not only that it allows pornographers to make hordes of money by writing trash, but that it simultaneously places so little value on culture that even the "successful" serious author often finds him or herself living well below the poverty line, struggling to survive through other kinds of part-time work.

Writers must be guardians of education, literacy, and culture in their own society. American writers need more than a national poet laureate salaried by Congress for a year at a time to meet this challenge. While it's a step in the right direction symbolically, we need to push for recognition of the value of a writer's labor in concrete terms. We also need a greater emphasis in American society on freedom of human enterprise rather than simply freedom of commercial enterprise.

Fortunately, American writers have the political freedoms needed to pursue a better lot for themselves and a lifting of cultural values for all Americans.

I can only hope that Soviet writers will keep pushing their government for the right to describe the world and reveal their vision freely.

Linda M. Wagner

Central Region V. P.

National Writers Union

Missed Moments

1985

I would caress you
If fate permitted
But despite the breezy flow of love
Pouring into my veins with the spring
The tide of time is out tonight
And your exhausted spirit
Has gently closed your eyes

At times we may as well
Be in separate, distant lands
The ache of desire
Can't be met and sprung free
Like a flying jay
Work is in the way
Amerikan style work is in the way

And what's this house and
What's the garden in our backyard
When they echo with emptiness?
I long for the giggle of a child
To become the rolling laughter
Of a person I watch growing up

When youth and its impatience tore at me
This moment would have burst
Into bitter biting frustration
Now it occasions a feeling not shared
A mutual joy not revealed
A freedom sadly caged

What I could give to you
If fate will only permit.

Late May 1985

I am pregnant!

September 18, 1985
Ending our last vacation B.C. (before children) in San Juan Islands off
Seattle coast
Growing large – life kicking and thrashing within me.
A natural, warm, and wonderful feeling.
Signs of hope in the future –
Long struggles, but signs of hope.

November 9, 1985
Now the "Dweezil" kicks,
Says, "I'm here,
You're not alone," and
There's comfort
In the movement
Watching my stomach jump and move
Like a shimmying bowl of Jello.
Like waves through the ocean.

Sunday, February 2, 1986
One week overdue.
Focusing: the main thing is I haven't had the baby.
What "all of it" is about is
Fear of death (the baby's or mine)

Fear of pain (bones splitting)
Fear of being out of control (C-section)
I want to get on with the baby's life.

1. Remember: you're both healthy now, all signs positive!

2. Nature takes her own sweet time. She'll let you know when it's time.

3. You're in good hands at Prucare and at home.

4. Imagine your cervix like a flower, opening slowly, and your healthy baby coming out!

Soon

Soon you will be the visible creation
Your tiny fists will stretch
Toward the skies
And your mouth will search
For the fountain of continued life.

Soon those who desired
To bring you into being
Through their acts of love
Will look upon you
Touch your tender skin
And speak quietly in your ears.

Soon the wonders and horrors,
Grandeurs and small joys,
All of sensation
Will be yours to learn
For the first time
Again.

Soon the hands and arms of love
Will enfold you,
Try to guide you in warmth
With shelter, food, and companionship
Through all of life's struggles.

We await you
Desiring to see and hear you
As you are.
We welcome you to this world
We are mom and dad.

March 13, 1986

Nathan is five weeks old. Next week I have my check-up and start working part-time on my consulting project.

He is beautiful. The emotion is like cold, brisk clean water from a rushing mountain stream. It cleanses and clarifies my life and world.

At the same time, I feel exhausted. My rhythms are set to Nathan's cries and smiles. His cry is lusty – powerful and demanding.

His eyes are bright dark, moist sponges, opening to the waters of visual sensation like a hand passing before his face, the bright contrasting colors of clowns, keys, and quilts.

His digestion is an ever-rumbling volcanic factory producing gases, liquids, and solids that put any chemistry lab to shame.

His breath is a snorting, squeaking struggle for life with bubbling coos that soothe and delight.

His suck is unequivocal and straightforward. When sated, it plays with the magic of touch, the skin-to-skin human contact we crave from birth.

(Later that day)

Your cries hurt more than just my ears
My gut and heart convulse
With each of your sobs
I try the diaper but it's clean and dry
I nurse and you turn away screaming
I whisper, "Relax, calm down,"
But your tiny limbs thrash
And your infant fist
Throws a mean left to my jaw.
Oh, how it hurts me
This seeming rejection
Of my overly anxious child.

Her First Child at Age 34

July 19, 1986

With each dress, skirt, or blouse she tried on, she felt youth oozing from the base of her feet. As she searched the mirror for a new image, the face of her child laughed back in an apparition just south of her groin.

Although she'd waved goodbye to those carelessly tossed teases and the consciously provocative style many years before the birth, she had somehow soothed her uncertainty about her sexual appeal in the interim with a glance at her tight, flat stomach and gently curved hips. Now, post-partum middle age, even graying temples, had befallen her in one swift motion like the theatrical swoosh of a fencing blade.

All around her at the gym, college-age girls giggled their neurotic self-possession. She recalled feeling that way long ago.

The time approached for her return home to family. She wanted just a few more moments to look for the new woman she'd become, but a tired husband and a hungry baby have little patience for self-indulgence. Five hours every three months, on a day or weekend. That's what parenthood allows for free-form reflection, if a mother is fortunate enough to have a cooperative husband or a babysitter.

"This is as good as it gets."

August 3, 1986

Sunday night on the swing on the back porch, overlooking a weeded garden. My wine glass still one-third full, while I hear the songs of locusts, crickets, a neighbor hammering new siding onto his home. My spouse sitting next to me reading the Sunday *New York Times* magazine. The baby asleep in his crib inside. I lose the compulsion to pick up the book review section and write this instead.

A former colleague used to say, "Wealth is the final refuge of the unimaginative." I suspect he was quoting someone else, but whom, I'm not sure.

Last night, we were in the company of the unimaginatively wealthy. I used to feel angry disdain toward them. Now I feel that way only toward a woman of that class who tried to woo away my spouse's affections while I was pregnant. She is a woman who climbed the corporate ladder to strut in a real fur coat she had bought herself. She awakened late to the power of her sexuality, but by her late 20s, she used it as part of her arsenal of aggressive business behavior.

With her coiffed blond hair, diamond earrings and gown with the plunging back, she thinks she has power over the man I love. I see her as she is - neither genuine nor credible.

I no longer have deep emotional ties to my socioeconomic class in the way I once did. But I do have such ties to my lover of 13 years, my spouse of nearly seven, the father of my child. She will see, I am not just "the wife." She will learn, I can fight. For myself, for my love, for my child.

August 8-9, 1986

Our home is invaded by a masked intruder. See the 2021 essay, "Still Seeking Justice Worth Restoring" in Decade V pieces.

January 23, 1987

I've had little time for journal entries or creative writing with an infant, freelance journalism, and the National Writers Union. But a tremendous sense of balance has arrived in my life and there's no need to feel negative or reflect negativity. With a babysitter I can trust, I've returned to more freelancing for NPR, and I'm encouraged by somewhat higher rates of compensation and a better editor.

I've realized there's still a residue of bad feeling surrounding my past years at NPR. I can chalk that up to too much coffee, insecurity, and a wandering sense of direction. Since then, I've given up coffee, spent two years in focusing therapy, and given birth to a wonderful child. I don't hesitate to say that the problems that led to my ominous feelings have been erased from my present life. A thank you to my therapist and a pat on my own back seem to be warranted.

I still don't earn good money, but I think that's a possibility within the next three years, depending on the opportunities and my feelings about mothering. The important thing is that I have no anxiety over it and fortunately, it has not been a necessity.

I've had some success finally with the union, and I'm ready to step into the background. And the local is ready for that too. Judith has developed a strong public sense of herself, and she has a good group behind her. I'm pleased at my successes despite the need to fight some hard battles this past year. I've stood up to those I had to confront.

And the joy of Nathan is so pacifying that I have few fears of our future together and an eagerness and readiness to help him grow. I sense that I have time in the future to accomplish other goals. God willing, I will live a long life with Barry at my side and a son who will outlive us both.

Nathan, at 18 Months

August 1987

He is a wonderful child –
A beautifully engaging smile
Twinkling eyes like his father
Very thoughtful
Expressive
But spunky too

He will not be pushed around easily
He'll know his own way and will.
A special child
Always climbing, working, trying
But aware of others too.

We love him so.

May 1986: A Reporter's Notes

The head of emergency planning
For Com Ed's nuclear plants
Must leave by noon for a CAT scan
His thin torso, fragile hair, sallow skin
And raspy voice give testimony
To the treatments
Fifteen years with the company
Expert in environmental sampling
Exposed to radiation?
I try to ask
But the P.R. flack's presence
Breaks the intimacy needed
The head of emergency planning
For Com Ed's nuclear plants
Just laughs when I ask
Can you really prevent panic
In the face of
A major nuclear meltdown?
He hints no, not really.
Go easy on me
Death sits at my elbow.

Poetic justice peers,
Imagining truth, not fact.
This is not the stuff of journalism.

Thinking & Writing & Research

1987

Life wreaks havoc upon all
That's why "Give peace a chance"
Is more than an anti-war chant.
My senior high school history text
Taught me to be a revolutionary
"The most revolutionary of activities...thinking," it said.
Now school is distant past
Academic life so long ago
Life has little profundity.
It's all a matter of paying the bills
Working, swimming upstream
To remain middle class.
Meaning in my life
Has taken
Sharp turns.
Writing was once motivated
By ambition to change
The course of human events.
Activism as feminism
And unionism
Had the same goals.
For a short while
It seemed the goal
Was Fame.

But making sacrifices for Fame
Seems a hollow well
No clear water at bottom, only shiny muck.
Writing just a doing
For me
To enjoy.
Other fantasies are illusion
There is only the act of writing
Here and now.
Or the joy of research
Twisting and turning down a long circuitous trail
Of facts, figures, details.
Getting lost in library stacks
Buried beneath
An avalanche of history.

More on Motherhood - July 14, 1988

A neighbor yells, "It's Bastille Day!" I manage to pick up the backpack, my purse, my carrying bag, and Nathan's stroller, walk up the stairs, and watch that Nathan doesn't fall down behind me. I consider it a monumental victory that Nathan is not whining, crying, or acting obnoxious when he reaches the top of the stairs. Tonight, I'm in luck. There are no battles with my toddler, I've already cooked dinner the night before, and the air conditioners are in the windows, ready to be turned on to defeat the 90-degree weather in Brooklyn.

Before getting myself into bed, I take a long look at my whole body in the mirror, my bulging stomach and sagging butt. At age 35 and a half, I am 20 pounds above my age 25 weight and out of shape, with little willpower to change that. I've grown tired of battling, whether with society, a boss, men, or my child. I eat, sleep, eliminate, care for my little one, satisfy my husband when I have energy, and work a full-time job with no housekeeper. We split the parenting, house chores, bringing home the bacon (although he brings home more of it.) We are equals. So it goes.

I haven't read a book, magazine, or heard a new record album in months. I've seen just one new movie lately (Bull Durham) which did not even get me that excited.

I no longer sense my own sensuality, perhaps because I'm overweight and out of shape. But I just don't care. I consider it amazing that I make it through the day without losing my cool.

Nathan is a joy – it is a deep, richly rewarding experience to be a parent. But it is demanding. I've had to mature a lot.

I haven't given up dreams of languorous hours reading book, making love, swimming alone, walking in the woods – those peaceful, quiet activities will be mine to do again one day...in 15 or 20 years...when I'm 55...

Then, I'll write my book, do more traveling, swim, and run, and be a mother too. And work will be that necessary activity that is prelude to life's real purpose – play.

But now, I have to get to sleep, be ready to wake up and be Nathan's mom, get us all ready, go to work, and keep going and going and going.

One Child Here, One on the Way

I look forward to my companion's return and sense his presence in his absence, as does our toddler son. Nathan requested, "A butterfly daddy" story and said, "Good night to daddy far away."

Nathan is the joy of it all – may he live a long life well beyond us. Now my creativity is with him, telling stories and making up songs for him.

He paints – this may be one mode of his expression, and athletics – he is so gifted all around. We will give him the rock bed. I believe Barry and I are strong enough and share a powerful enough love to withstand what comes our way.

Here in Brooklyn

In 1988
Working full-time
I want a calmer life
For me, my son
And another child

With time to speculate
Write
Lounge
And play with my children

At 36 years, I am no longer desiring the reporter's life but seeking a quieter, more contemplative life. They say depression is caused by too realistic an outlook, by admitting one's real limitations. Creative success is drive, they say, by an ego blind to its faults. In that sense, insensitive to the needs of others.

I don't accept that, but that battle seems too often like a lost one.

I'm thinking of my son, my husband, my parents, my husband's parents, my siblings, friends, colleagues. My nation? Not now – the political phase of my life is behind me. I no longer feel comfortable in that sphere.

October 18, 1988

I'm reading Gail Sheehy's "Pathfinders" to learn how to become one, only to discover that, according to her criteria, I already am one. I've just come out of a fairly depressed and insecure period, during which I bought this book.

I had the evening alone with Nathan. What a sweetheart he is. At age two years, eight months, he's begun to talk with me about things that have bothered or frightened him. It's such an important step, that he can ask about emotional reactions and I can verbally reassure him, in addition to physically reassuring him.

Parent magazine's article on fears was also helpful in getting me to understand my own role in eliciting fearful reactions. Child development is hard to follow without an outside framework for understanding it.

Pregnant with #2

November 21, 1988

A friend asks for wicca wisdom
Of childbirth, blood, sleep gained and lost
Those fundamentals like
"How often will I go to the bathroom
Will I get a shower today,
Can I eat?"

She suspected a "conspiracy of silence"
But it's only that our childless friends
Won't take time to listen
To the cries of newborn babies
And the anguish of their parents
They block out real life
Until it bowls them over like pins at the alley.

Sleep, sweet sleep
Sweet, sweet sleep
And dreams...

I say a prayer and brew this brew for you
To lull your babe to sleep
And give you peace, rest,
And the future.

Quotes from Nathan, February 1989, age 3 with a pregnant mom

(Instead of upstate NY) "Upstairs New York"

"How do you get the baby out? You have to use a wrench...a pliers,...a hammer."

"Do the midwives have a mop?"

"...The street sweeper streets the swee...streets the...the street sweeper <u>cleans</u> the street."

March 5, 1989

I will be 37 after the baby is born.

Voluptuousness is the sensation of my pregnancy now – a full feeling – the lower abdominal muscles straining to hold the growing weight of my belly. I've gained about six pounds, maybe seven, so far. My breasts, though still small, have the feeling of fullness. After an epic of exhaustion, I am beginning to feel rested. I am beginning to sense light and warmth.

Knowing that Bar and Nathan are doing well in my absence makes me feel more rested and easy about being here. I dream of them, of sweet love making with Bar; of fearing that Nathan is lost, only to discover him as a baby on Barry's back.

Today, with my parents, I began to feel my own rhythms, for the first time in a while, all this while helping to sort and pack and clean and move.

My dad is struggling with so much now. Mom is very patient with the situation – her sleep is key. My oldest sister Joan and I do sister-things – worry jointly about Mom and Dad; compare the little bumps we both have on our heads, talk about children, husbands, health, birth, sickness, death.

The big issues. Religion, some cautiously. The unshared religion. But sharing faith – now, that's another story.

August 9, 1989

Buried in my belly is a new life about to show its face. A world of possibilities, opening, creations, joys – oh, sufferings too – I recall those sleepless infant nights…

Yet this child will live and grow – healthy, strong, enduring. This child has already borne great stress, keeping a strong steady heartbeat and exhibiting generous movement despite its cramped quarters.

I love Nathan so fiercely because we waited for him so long. This child I love so fiercely because it is comfort from my grief at life's miserable endings.

And some grief (over my own mom and dad) must escape now. I must avoid a crash of my spirits after the birth.

1988- 1989

Orphaned with Living Parents

10/30/1988 - Before the Stroke

Every so often when talking about wills, living trusts, nursing homes and cemetery plots, every so often it hits me that what we're discussing is the disability and death of my father and/or mother. And the underlying pain of it all, of losing some part of my inner core, just rests on my mind with a weight like lead, asbestos, radioactive isotopes, or chemical weapons.

I try to keep the discussion contained to certain hours, after Nathan's bedtime, before my own, only to lose sleep and comfort. Just as I may forget that Barry is in the midst of a trial, he forgets that I'm consumed by these concerns.

With a toddler in toilet "teaching," all of it just pushes the tenuous over the brink. My child is feeling the stress of his major passage from diapers to underpants and potty, feeling success, failure, fear, confidence. And their mother, with ambivalence about everything, is feeling very shaky about her own parents.

My dad, meanwhile, is unable to talk on the phone.

Return from Rome, NY

February 20, 1989

The stench of stale cigarette smoke
Baked between the fibers of my robe,
My towels, my coat
Every piece of clothing emptied
From my suitcase
Stinks of it.
The blare of television volume
Permeating every room in the house
Boxing matches
Jeopardy
60 Minutes
Golf, bowling, football
Nature shows and sitcoms
And Jeopardy
My dad's in jeopardy
And he's not on the TV
He's under it
It's choking the life
Squeezing the sanity
Emptying the humanity
From my father.

Paternity Insanity

What can we learn
From this pale, pale human shadow
Who can't recall that his daughter
Is not his granddaughter?
Who holds a yardstick in his hand
One moment to use it
And the next, forgets why it's there
Or what it does?

What can we learn
From this shouting paranoiac
Who insists that his children
Are taking advantage of him,
Then turns the TV volume so high
That all reality is drowned,
Including those children?

What can we learn
From this great-grandfather child
Now that we've come to accept
That this is what the man has become?

After Mom's First Stroke

July 1989 in New Hampshire, after the hospital in Syracuse

The moon rises
Pulls the tides
Seasons pass
First lacking confidence
Then gaining it
Then leaking confidence
Into the great beyond
Control once apparent
Now a child's concern.
Streams of consciousness
Once assumed
Now lost in a flow of blood.
Who will care? (we all will)
Who will bear the load
None of us know.
Still fettered by anxiety
Wanting to touch home base
With sorrow purged and healed.
But tonight
Unable to cope
Or see the light of hope.

Guilt over the luxury of distance
From the crisis even though
They said go
Don't worry yourself
As a birth draws near.
Who has that power of strength?
Who is the parent
And who the child now?
What place is mine on this team?

After the Stroke, in the Nursing Home

October 12, 1989

My mother and father are like Jeanette Mc Donald and Nelson Eddy, perched upon their isolated mountaintops, calling out to each other across vast canyons of dead and scarred brain tissue.

Mom says, "They said I'm not eating well, but I just don't like the "jodgie." Her eyes roll toward the ceiling, aware that the point she was trying to make was obliterated by her inability to find the right word at the right and crucial time. "Jodgie," she repeats in a tone of self-disgust and defeat. "I just don't know," she says, over and over, with an inflection that her children know means, "I just want to give up."

Meanwhile, dad asks his daughter through tears of incomprehension, "What does she mean, 'Jodgie'? Does that mean something? Why can't she talk?" As if he were a three-year-old child whose mother just died, the perpetual "why" upon his lips. In fact, his mother had died 69 years ago, when he was only seven, and the echoes of that pain racked his modestly demented mind as he faced the shell of my mother, his wife of 50 years.

My seven-week-old baby lies upon the bed in the nursing home, my mother smiling and cooing at her from her nearby wheelchair, pleased at her ability to communicate effectively with this totally dependent infant. Baby Joanna responds with bright eyes and broad smiles to the soft, high-pitched voice that still flows from her grandma with ease. My sorrow is lessened, transformed to contentment, even happiness. My mother can still laugh, enjoy, and give to my daughter, even while imprisoned in a half-dead body, a half-crippled brain.

"Not what she was, not what she was," the refrain begins to fade from my consciousness as I see mom, despite her illness, more enthralled with this baby girl than she was with my firstborn while healthy. I hear in my mind the phrase from Bonnie Raitt's latest release, *Nick of Time*:

> "Life gets mighty precious
>
> When there's less of it to waste."

November 1989 – Motherhood Better Before 30? (Unpublished)

In response to "Motherhood's Better Before 30" by Kim C. Flodin, NYTimes 11/2/1989

I salute Kim Flodin's desire to have children at age 27 and build on feminist struggles of the past. But I think she needs to be better educated about the complexity of struggles and the plethora of reasons that many older women like me delayed their childbearing.

I, for one, have not climbed any corporate ladders. But before having children, I needed to feel hope about the future. I cannot overstate this point.

A severely negative psychological impact upon women (and men) who came of age in the 1960s and early '70s was caused by the news of many tragedies of those times: the Vietnam War; rising divorce rates; the appearance of vast numbers of impoverished displaced homemakers; virulent racism; the proliferation of nuclear weapons, power plants and radioactive waste; environmental disasters. News of these and many other horrors of history were just surfacing in the news media when I was a young teen. They left me and many of my contemporaries at a delicately impressionable age paralyzed by a fear for the future of the human race.

It took many years for me and many of my friends to overcome that fear, to feel confident that the human race could meet the challenges before us, to believe that any children we have will have a future. It took activism - working to change things - to gain that confidence.

Now, on both personal and broadly philosophical and political levels, the hope that I've regained is invested in my children. They are symbols of my faith in humanity's ability to confront and overcome its own follies. They are my hope.

Perhaps Kim has never experienced the depths of despair that we encountered. Perhaps we've helped her and her contemporaries to feel the hope and faith necessary to desire children. May she never feel such despair. May she succeed in her efforts. May she have beautiful, healthy children, a supportive spouse, and a safe world where they all can grow and build upon the past.

Mid-1985 Linda with NPR Chicago Bureau atop the Carbon & Carbide Building in downtown Chicago. In this photo, Linda is pregnant with her firstborn.

December 1988 – Linda with her Wagner family at her parents' 50th wedding anniversary party. In this photo, Linda is pregnant with her second-born.

August 1989 – Linda with her babies.

DECADE III: 1990 - 1999

Early Middle Years: Age 38 - 47

Maternal Concerns & Consumer and Patients' Rights

I had always loved the soulful spiritual, "Sometimes I Feel Like a Motherless Child." In 1990, with my three-year-old son and new infant whose grandmother - my mother - remained incapacitated in a nursing home, I found that the song had a freshly painful meaning. Most of us hope that our children will bring sweet joy into our parents' lives. My parents, now so disabled, were unable to appreciate their roles as grandparents to my children, even though they had been happy in those roles for nearly a dozen older grandkids borne by my siblings. (See "Mother's Day at the Nursing Home.")

Fortunately, my son and daughter had Grandma and Grandpa from my husband's side, and plenty of aunts and uncles from both sides to provide guidance and role models, aside from the roles that Barry and I played as parents. In addition, they both came to have many wonderful adults in their lives who provided childcare and education for our family.

I had hoped to maintain a part-time work life for a longer period while my children were young. But we had underestimated the dramatic increase in living costs when we moved to New York City. I left a job at the Brooklyn Historical Society before my daughter was born. But they called me back as a consultant when my replacement, soon after he started the job, developed serious complications from an AIDS infection, an occurrence all too common among gay men at the time.

Even that unexpected consulting income did not cover our ordinary expenses. To avoid bankruptcy, I had to get a full-time salary that would cover childcare costs and provide enough net household income to complement that of my spouse and meet all our other expenses. Quality early childcare was — and still is — revolutionary for working mothers, but it is also expensive, both financially and emotionally. Few feelings are as wrenching as sending your very young children to full-time day care, no matter how excellent that care may be. In pieces included in this decade's collection, I share some of these struggles.

During the spring of 1990, I accepted a full-time job at Consumers Union (CU), the nonprofit parent organization that publishes *Consumer Reports* (*CR*), whose headquarters was in the process of moving from Mount Vernon to Yonkers, within the same Westchester County just north of the Bronx. For about four months, I commuted one hour each way from Brooklyn's Park Slope neighborhood to Westchester County and back, while relying on a wonderful older woman named Lena to care for the baby and pick up our son from pre-school. My salary was nearly twice what I had made at the Brooklyn Historical Society, high enough to cover the childcare costs that first year and meet our minimum credit-card payments for things like clothing, while my husband's salary covered most of the basics of rent, utilities, and food.

The commute proved to be too much for a mother of two young children, so we planned to move north from New York City to the Hudson River village of Dobbs Ferry, New York after CU moved its headquarters to nearby Yonkers. Our move from Park Slope that summer was far from simple. Due to a collapse in the co-op apartment market in New York City that followed the stock market crash of October 1987, it was impossible for any potential buyer to get a mortgage for our 12th Street railroad flat, despite its backyard garden and highly desirable Brooklyn neighborhood, just a block from Prospect Park. We found an interested buyer who agreed to rent the apartment, but at a rate that did not cover our mortgage. For a year, until co-op mortgages became available to these buyers once again, we rented our apartment to them at a loss. When our renters were finally able to make the purchase, we had to borrow $5,000 to close the deal. If we had been able to keep the apartment, we might have enjoyed the dramatic escalation in its value – now, in 2022, about ten times what we paid in 1987.

In Dobbs Ferry, we found a first-floor apartment in a duplex on a busy road that led into the village. It was just a 15-minute drive from my office, at a time when nearly all employers required employees to work on site. So, I was able to spend more time during weekday mornings and evenings with my children, a priority I had set for my family life. Dobbs Ferry was – and remains — a community with excellent public schools, pre-school childcare, easy walkability, and the beauty of the Hudson River. It has a Metro North train stop, making it an easier commute for my husband to lower Manhattan. It seemed to be the ideal place to raise children.

We found a respected pre-school there for our four-year-old son, and we were very fortunate to find a young married couple without children of their own who wanted to bring Joanna, at the age of nearly one year, into their home while I was at work. The husband was a local police officer, and the wife had been a fitness coach. They cared for Jo as if she was their own child, getting her hair trimmed, taking her for photos, feeding her the healthiest foods, and ensuring she had plenty of outdoor physical play.

After that type of attention, it was emotionally wrenching to move Joanna at age two to the group day care center across the road from my office in Yonkers, NY. With Nathan now in public school, this step offered our baby girl interaction with other children and adults and an enriched indoor and outdoor play environment, while it reduced our costs and ensured that I was close at hand in the event of any emergencies.

On the work front at Consumers Union, I began learning the history and present-day activities of a different type of revolutionary change catalyst, an advocacy that some in the American business and political worlds consider radical. The rights of consumers in an intensely individualized capitalist society are difficult to guarantee. Consumers Union started in 1936 within the cooperative and labor union movements of the 1930s, dedicated to protecting household purchasers from scams and dangerous products. These broader movements led to many bloody conflicts between workers and consumers on one side and the owners and enforcers of capital on the other side. I was excited to be a part of a historic movement for consumers in the marketplace and the courts. In addition, I was hired into a union job, represented in 1990 by the Newspaper Guild. The Newspaper Guild web site describes CU's origins:

> *"In 1935, the staff of Consumer's Research Magazine struck for the right to form a union and when the strikers were beaten down by management, they formed their own company, Consumers Union of the United States. Some of the company's seed money was provided by the labor movement. Heywood Broun, a founder of The Newspaper Guild, was on CU's original Board of Directors.*
>
> *The first issue of Consumer Reports was published in May of 1936 and responded to the question about if it was being published to benefit consumers or workers saying: "By reporting on labor conditions under which consumer goods are produced, by letting consumers know what products are manufactured under good labor conditions so that when possible they can favor them in making their purchases; by letting them know what products are produced under unfair conditions so that consumers can avoid such products, Consumers Union hopes to add what pressure it can to fight for higher wages and for unioniza- tion and the collective bargaining which are labor's bulwark against declining standards of living ... The only way in which any organi- zation can aid them materially as consumers is by helping them, in their struggle as workers, to get an honest wage."*

From the 1990s through today, *Consumer Reports* and its parent organi- zation, Consumers Union, have grown tame as compared to its radical origins, when it faced accusations of being a Communist front in the 1930s and '40s. And yet its core values of consumer protection, along with many decades bat- tling for reforms in health care, insurance, and other financial services, have had a significant impact on the safety of consumer products and the fairness of consumer services for purchasers in the USA and around the world. I was glad to be part of CU in the 1990s when it was led by a strong woman, Rhoda H. Karpatkin, who was really the only mentor I had during my entire career.

In 1990, CR was a printed magazine. By 1996, it added an online publication that eventually became the organization's "cash cow." I was fortunate to be on the internal team that planned for that success. I worked alongside, and eventually hired and led a team of highly productive professionals who kept an extremely positive view of Consumer Reports and consumers' rights in the forefront of the news. I initiated the availability of CR's information in Spanish, both in the form of translated, syndicated radio content for Spanish-language stations, as well as through radio and TV interviews with native Spanish speakers – one from Panama, and another from Puerto Rico - whom I hired as public information specialists. I fully embraced the CU philosophy that I was "doing well by doing good."

However, Dobbs Ferry was a near suburb of New York City, and that meant expensive housing and real estate taxes, and a broad range of wealth among its residents, with everyone from sanitation workers to hedge fund managers. It required a lot of assets and income to maintain a middle-class lifestyle there without some government subsidy. Furthermore, being a renter in a community of homeowners led some Dobbs Ferry mothers to shun our family after their sons' play dates with our son showed them where we lived.

Our excellent public schools were a major reason for the high property taxes in Dobbs Ferry, since that is how the schools were funded in our state. The education that both Nathan and Joanna received, and the generally safe character of the community was worth every cent. When it became clear that our salaries would not make it feasible to buy a home in our new community, despite the significant increase in my income, Barry left the District Attorney's office to join a risk management practice at a major accounting firm in a highly compensated partnership position. In addition, I accepted a move from a union position to a management role. By 1994, we were able to purchase a home, but, once again, we had to borrow from a sibling to make the required down payment, even though it was only 5% of the buying price – at that time, $300,000 for a 3-bedroom raised ranch built in 1957.

We found ourselves in a delightful neighborhood filled with younger and older children. Our mayor's home was just up the block, and we were tucked away from traffic. We had finally reached a financial stage where we didn't need to find pennies to pay all the bills. Our children were making friends, doing well in school, and enjoying plenty of sports indoor and outside. We loved our neighbors and the parents we met through the school and sports teams, and we were able to afford luxuries like piano lessons, art supplies, sporting gear, and vacations to Disneyland in California and Estes Park, Colorado and New Mexico, even some overseas travel to Europe with the kids.

Not long after I became a manager in CR's Public Information Office, CU faced scorched-earth litigation by the car company, Suzuki, whose lawyer claimed that CR auto testers had faked tests showing one of its SUV models tipping over. I was assigned to be the communications director on the litigation team, where I proudly defended the role of consumer information and advocacy in the court of American public opinion for a very long decade. But my work life came to demand more from me personally than I was able to manage well.

By my mid-40s, I had grown exhausted, with dry skin and hair, and began to feel the symptoms of perimenopause. At a certain point, I felt, quite physically, that something had clicked off within my body. I developed heart palpitations, and after numerous scans, tests, and treatment efforts proved ineffective, my primary care doctor ordered new blood tests and diagnosed me with hypothyroidism. That internist, Dr. David Goldberg, explained to me that the medical practice had discovered that chronic exhaustion and unmanaged stress keep cortisol levels in our bloodstream turned on so high that it could break down parts of the endocrine system. In me, this had triggered a malfunction of the thyroid gland, no longer able to produce sufficient hormones to regulate my metabolism. Without corrective medication, I was at risk of serious illness, including the slowing down of my heart and brain function and eventual coma. Ever since then, I have taken thyroid medication religiously, with blood tests at least annually to check my thyroid hormone levels.

I began to think about early retirement from a full-time job to manage my stress, have more time with our family, and pursue some other interests such as writing, piano, perhaps even a return to radio production. This was not to be for many more years. Even though Barry did well at the firm, they brought in a heavier-hitting rainmaker above him with wealthier contacts. This did not sit well with Barry, who was not convinced he would be kept in the partnership, and he made a plan to begin his own practice. In the course of that transition, he miscalculated his tax obligations from the accounting firm partnership. We were suddenly deeply in debt to the IRS and New York State, which forced us to refinance with a cash-out mortgage to pay the taxes. While establishing his own practice, Barry's income dropped at the same time that we incurred heavy new financial responsibilities.

My dreams of an earlier retirement and preparing for college costs evaporated. Within a year, Barry landed on his feet, as he always did, and was offered a position with a risk management firm. In addition, I received promotions with salary increases that helped to stabilize our situation. But the rich gravy train had left us behind. We canceled an overseas trip, reduced what expenses we could, and made it clear to the kids that some luxuries they wanted, such as the pricey private school that Joanna begged to attend, were simply out of the question.

Despite all the financial, work-related, and health struggles of the 1990s, I had the great pleasure of mothering two amazing children, and the love of a devoted spouse. Together we decided to join the very reform Temple Beth Shalom, despite the fact that I am not Jewish and did not feel right about converting. Our children attended Hebrew School to have some anchor of religious perspective in a world filled with all types of believers and non-believers. I was an active member of the Dobbs Ferry PTSA, and Barry was eventually voted onto the School Board. We enjoyed Halloween parties in our little neighborhood, featuring a haunted house, costume contest, and talent show. We had the joys of discovering how much our children learned in every aspect of life from us, each other, teachers, coaches, and friends and neighbors. In general, life was very kind to our young family, and we were blessed in many ways.

Regarding some of the pieces I wrote during this decade:

- In 1991, when my son was five and my daughter was nearly two years old, I wrote a poem/prayer included in this section. I found it in 2021, while cleaning out old files. I am no Amanda Gorman, but I was surprised that I might have written it yesterday, with my grandkids in mind.

- In his later years, my father had a combination of Alzheimer's Disease, heart disease, diabetes, and emphysema. He smoked cigarettes until he forgot what a cigarette was. Despite our disagreements when I was younger, I grieved deeply over the gradual and then final loss of my dad. However, his death made sense. But soon after he died, I learned of the tragically senseless murder/suicide involving the boy who had lived next door to me, a boy with whom I played as a child. See the personal essay, "The End of the Boy Next Door. Sadly, there are too many deaths that make no sense and raise only questions. One of the greatest questions is why we allow so many people in our nation to die by gun violence. If ever there was a need for a revolution, it is for a nonviolent, regulatory American Revolution to neuter the power of the NRA and gun lobby, and to stop the intentional distortion of the Second Amendment by opponents of common-sense gun safety laws. If ever there was a need for bold, dramatic change inside our homes, it is in those homes where domestic violence thrives, unchallenged.

- In the mid-1990s, a documentary series produced in the U.K. and titled **Watergate: The Corruption and Fall of Richard Nixon** was broadcast in the U.S. My children were then aged nine and six, and I watched the series at home, during a period when cable TV news was just gaining serious traction. The bursting of television screens into the living rooms of American homes was a dramatic revolution during the 1950s, one that had an enormous impact on my early years and our family dynamic. The spread of cable television and the introduction of the internet in the 1990s produced another revolution in the information and entertainment consumption of American and global audiences. Watching a documentary on Nixon produced by British television revived painful memories of traumas that have affected the psyches of millions of now-older Americans who were sometimes united but often torn asunder. After watching that chunk of video history, I wrote an essay about it in 1995. The divisions in American society that exploded in the 1960s and early 1970s live on today within our national DNA. The sentiments and beliefs expressed in that essay, sharing echoes of my feelings from 20 years earlier, resurfaced with a vengeance in 2015, more than four decades after I first experienced them.

PIECES WRITTEN BETWEEN 1990 - 1999

On Letting the Past Go – 1990

14 years after leaving Lexington, KY

I remember coming home from my job at WLAP in 1976, which I both loved and hated. Loved, because of the challenge of writing for money, because of the paycheck for a professional task, mostly because I saw a chance to grow. Hated, because it was the real world of commercial bubble gum rock and roll – music I dislike, people who were too different from me. Nonetheless, I knew I could learn good things there.

I remember coming home to a very depressed Barry – he sat with his pen in hand, describing to me the "fictional" scenario he was writing – about two lovers who decide to kill themselves together. I saw suicide written in his eyes and longed to see the carefree, joyful youth I'd known only months before.

So, I went with him, with his plans, I loved him so. Of course, he does not remember it the way I do, because I did not share what I really felt and thought at the time.

I gave up a dream of going to Journalism school at Berkely or staying in radio in Lexington, all the time believing I could make my own way, that I had what it takes, thinking I would be able to get a career-type job in one of the country's most depressed cities – Buffalo, New York.

I made my way, all right, into an underpaid field, where I, at least, felt at home. I love the music, the people, the potential.

All in all, it is this powerful love that so few people find, that has kept us bound together. Sometimes the binds chafe, there's no denying that. But it's well worth any occasional aggravation and doubt, much of which is self-doubt, I must add.

Barry is still that wonderful, joyful, youth inside, when we get the chance to unearth him and me from all the intervening years and stresses. Others tell me they see that youth in our son Nathan and our daughter Joanna now. Although I must take some credit for that myself, I know how much Barry has contributed to the sparkle in their eyes, the giggle in their voices, the gentleness in their souls.

May 1990 – MOTHER'S DAY AT THE NURSING HOME

Each time I see her there
My mother's ears grow larger,
Her face smaller,
Her limp right side presses against death,
While an unschooled left hand crawls "mom"
On birthday cards to her children,
And lifts a cup of pudding to her mouth to lick
As if it were an ice cream cone.

There was, once upon a time, a bitterness
In her – at my blue jeans, work shirts,
And unshaven legs,
Caustic critiques of the barren roads
Down which I rode my identity,
So antithetical to hers –
So lush with natural vegetation and waterways –
Or so it seemed, once upon a time.

And a bitterness in me
At her narrow vision of beauty in a girl
With a smaller nose than mine
And wavier, redder hair than mine,
And a suppler mind than mine –
That I was always, to her,
Other, except in those moments
When we shared the chains of gender.

But that was in her menopause,
My adolescence,
Time shaded by the dark vengeance
Of hormonal centuries
Of our foremothers' historically frustrated memories
That we had not been able
To live up to our expectations
Of ourselves and each other
However vastly differently we defined
"having it all."

That was once upon a time,
And this is now.
I sit beside her heart whose rhythm is propelled
By a small mechanical device under her skin
My own heartbeat made irregular by some infection
In its valve
I feel the loss of sleep I've suffered
Since my own daughter was born,
The sicknesses, the fears
But also, the wonder.

When my baby girl was in utero, my body fed her these lessons.
The DNA in my chromosomes told her
About the history of a woman's place
Fluctuations in my hormones, blood pressure,
Mood and pace sent clear signals –
A childbearing woman has fits and starts,
Fits and starts, fits and starts.
The future depends on this,
Humankind must give in
At home, on the job, in the streets,
Or life, itself, is in jeopardy.

Why Not Childcare Loans on Same Terms as Student Loans?
Published in *The New York Times*, May 5, 1991

To the Editor:

My husband and I fairly well fit the New York City family portrait in your article on two-paycheck families (The Week in Review, April 21), but we have two children under kindergarten age, a boy who just turned 5, a girl at 20 months. Our annual childcare costs about $20,000. For the reasons you state, I work full time – economic necessity, protection against financial dependence on my husband, as well as the feeling of self-worth a paycheck brings and the respect from others (husbands included) that a professional salary brings.

But after looking at the finances, I've had my doubts. I believe childcare is a family expense. Both parents are responsible for the care of the children, and men should not be let off the hook. What's the answer? Look to the model of student loans for college-age kids. Preschool childcare expenses are concentrated in a five-year span. Why not offer long-term, low-interest financing for preschool childcare?

The alternative is the route my husband and I have been forced to take – pay for childcare from disposable income, while accumulating credit card debt at 20 percent interest, based on three-year payback (that has paid for clothing, car repair and other routine expenses). I wish we had been able to borrow on the terms of my husband's student loans – 10-year payback at 7 to 12 percent, with no penalty for early payment on more of the principal.

We would finish off the debt, just in time for college tuition. But perhaps we would have managed to sock away savings for that if our childcare costs in the early years had been spread over a longer period.

I would add that I see this as a model only because we have free public school available for kindergarten to 12th grade but not for earlier preschool years, at least not in most places.

LINDA WAGNER

Dobbs Ferry, N.Y., (sent) April 21, 1991

July 10, 1991

From application to Bright Horizons for Joanna's entry to group pre-school at age two

Began walking at 14 months, Talking at 10 months.

Special words: "Juice" a drink, "eat" when she's hungry; "Bobbie" her special blanket.

How do you handle fussy times/tantrums? Leave her alone, but stand within sight, she usually stops and comes over for comfort when she's done.

Child's favorite toy? Anything that requires putting things in and taking them out.

Plays with her brother in evening – lots of physical play 7-8 pm. Bath 7:45 pm. Bed 8-8:15 pm.

Parenting philosophy: We want our children to grow at their own pace and develop their unique strengths with guidance that is clear, nurturing, and compassionate. We want them to have the chance to develop every facet of themselves – physical, intellectual, emotional, social, moral/spiritual.

A Parent's Prayer to the Memory of God

Aug. 9, 1991

"Faith is an island. in the setting sun,
But proof is the bottom line for everyone." - Paul Simon

Meaning must be more than song lyrics
Heard on headphones during a morning walk,
More than dreams of a boss you pray to escape.
It is a child whose cry drives us to tears
Cresting on the twining of hopes
Into younger, stronger drives.

And where is their future?
In international banks for drug dealers, terrorists, and twisted intelligence?
On hospital wards filled with dying AIDS patients?
In schools brimming with the brain-damaged babes of crack addicts?
On the streets with no jobs, no homes, no hope?

Oh, give us a leader with a mind as fresh and sharp
As a new microchip in a state-of-the-art communications network,
All the bugs worked out.
With a heart as pure as a toddler's
And a will as strong as an ocean wave
Driven by high winds blowing in every direction.

We have no more room for error.
We need proof, dear God,
We need proof.

On the Clarence Thomas/Anita Hill hearing

October 1991

In matters of sexual impropriety, the male response of denial is as inbred as the reflex to cover his testicles when physically threatened. Ask any woman who has had her suspicions of a mate's infidelity persistently denied until she literally walks in and catches him in the act, whatever the "act" may be.

A man's sexual impropriety and lies go together. Why should anyone be surprised that a man would lie to protect himself when accused, especially if there is no way for the accuser to prove what has happened?

It's the nature of the beast. Paul Simon captured it eloquently.

"Still a man hears what he wants to hear

And disregards the rest."

And a woman hears what she does not want to hear and is unable to disregard it.

This is the truth. It explains the entire Senate scenario of Anita Hill testifying about the improper conduct of Clarence Thomas. And it explains why the discomfort and public discussion will not go away.

The End of the Boy Next Door

I last saw Ronnie at a teen dance at St. Matthew's Elementary School while I was visiting East Syracuse for the weekend. From our births to age 12, we'd been next door neighbors in this upstate railroad town, where soot from coal trains coated the windowsills and the number of Christian churches was rivalled only by that of taverns.

Ronnie, at age 14, looked handsome as ever, with his tanned face, sandy brown and blond hair cropped short, and characteristically twinkling blue eyes. It had been about two years since I'd moved away. Now, in our awkward early teen years, we exchanged few words when we encountered each other. But broad grins broke across our faces, like sunrise across the horizon.

The first time I ever got into real trouble, I was with Ronnie on a summer afternoon in 1956. Both of us as four-year-olds, we were playing unsupervised in our safe, quiet, small-town backyards. Ronnie's aunt and uncle, who lived in the upstairs back apartment of their three-family house, were out for the day. They had locked their door, but the porch window was wide open. We climbed up the stairs and through the window.

We played with everything we could reach. We put lipstick all over the mirrors and face powder all over the floor. We left the refrigerator door open and the water running in the bathtub. We turned on the radio (no TV in our neighborhood yet) to WNDR, blasting with songs by Johnny Mathis and the Andrews Sisters.

Soon after we hoisted ourselves back out through the window, Ronnie's relatives discovered the mayhem. His mother called my mother, who puzzled over this outrageous act by her usually reserved, well-behaved daughter. "Linda, what in the world got into you?" she asked, sitting in the kitchen behind me, brushing my hair. "You just went along with Ronnie, didn't you?"

Yes, I went along with Ronnie, who told me the following day, "I got whipped. What happened to you?" He was incredulous that my parents had merely given me "a good talking to."

My dad worked long hours six days a week and rarely had occasion to be the disciplinarian. That role fell to my mother, who used time-out in the back bedroom as punishment. If she even raised her voice to me, I crumbled and cried.

But in Ronnie's house, yelling was routine, and beatings came and went. His mom and dad had married in their late teens and had four kids – three of them boys – within four years. All six were quite good looking, all a little "on the wild side" by my family's standards. Despite their raucousness, no one ever told me to shun our neighbors. That just wasn't done in our village in those days.

At about age seven, Ronnie got some type of fever and was so ill that everyone in the neighborhood whispered, "He just might not make it." When the contagion was past, his mom asked if I would come over to visit. She thought that seeing his friends might speed up his recovery. I can still see his face, white as a sheet against the pillow, resting on their living room couch, his voice too weak to speak. And I can still feel the joy upon hearing that he was finally "taking nourishment" and getting better.

But as boys and girls do at around age eight or nine, we drifted apart. Ronnie was the boy who kicked me off the baseball field when the kids on my block, overwhelmingly male, decided, "Girls are stupid and don't belong in our game." He also grabbed my hand in the darkness of his basement and made me touch his "thing" as initiation into the neighborhood club that met in his garage attic. I grew to despise him and wrote in my fifth-grade diary, "I hate boys!!!" with Ronnie in mind.

Yet, when I saw him at that summer dance, I felt strong love and warmth. Ronnie and I had caught pollywogs, climbed trees, jumped into piles of autumn leaves, built forts, and shot marbles together on the soggy ground of fresh spring days, year after year. We played doctor at age five with other neighborhood kids

In the front room of my house when my mom and grandma were busy, and all the older siblings were out at school or work.

Born in the same year, we shared birthday celebrations. Ronnie's mother always baked special prizes like pennies or candy inside the birthday cake, warning us to be careful to feel and look for them. Ronnie even brought me to a service at his Episcopal Church, an event that made me seriously doubt my church's teaching that only those souls baptized Catholic would make it to heaven.

I knew that Ronnie's parents sometimes drank and fought, and that he idealized tough guys on motorcycles, like his uncle. But we were children together in the 1950s, a time of American optimism and supposed innocence.

My family moved on and out of a village declared "poverty-stricken" during the LBJ years. My dad reached middle-class affluence by taking a risk and buying his own grocery store 50 miles away, where he was very successful.

Ronnie finished high school and remained in East Syracuse. Now and then, my brother, who lived on the same block where we had grown up, told me that Ronnie had gotten into this trouble or that – never anything major.

Eventually Ronnie married a local girl, but never gave up chasing other women. He went to work for a local company and joined the volunteer fire department, the ultimate men's club in my hometown. Since before we'd been born, the highlight of every summer in East Syracuse was Firemen's Field Days, when the mobile amusement park came to the village and there was a contest between two teams of firemen holding hoses, blasting water at each other.

The last story I heard about Ronnie was told by my brother in his kitchen, where my family had gathered just after my father died. We planned to spend the next day greeting former neighbors at the wake and chatted about which neighbors we might see. I reluctantly embraced my dad's death at age 79, his relief from months and years of anguish, fear, and incapacitation due to Alzheimer's Disease and other chronic illnesses. My father's end was a long, sad decline, but it made sense after a long and full life.

But the final tale my brother shared about Ronnie has an air of unreality to me. I can't put my arms around it, and I can't quite let it go.

Just a few weeks earlier, Ronnie had taken a powerful shotgun outside a local bar, knowing his estranged wife was inside. He waited in his car until she came out with her girlfriends, and with blast after blast, he cut her down, literally ripping her body to shreds. Then he turned the gun on himself and blew his brains out.

My father's death left me with a type of peace. But Ronnie's death left me with puzzles I can't piece back together, with sorrows and fears that steal my sleep.

I always thought Ronnie was just a mixed-up kid who needed someone to straighten him out. Maybe the firemen thought of him that way too, when they hung the firehouse flag at half-mast after the murder/suicide, outraging many women in the village.

Ronnie, after all, had planned to kill his wife, a woman who, I heard, finally gave up on him and sent him on his way; a woman whom, I now imagine, Ronnie may have beaten, abused, and humiliated for many years.

I don't know with any certainty why it went this way. All I know is that I'm all grown up now. My childhood memories are suddenly loaded with grief, tangled like the vines and sour like the grapes in my old backyard. And the question, "How will my story end?" lingers with a threat it never seemed to have before.

Encouraged by My Dad from Beyond the Grave

July 12, 1992

Three months shy of age 40. I see Tina at age 38 as Senior Editor in Chief of The New Yorker, after holding the same position at Vanity Fair.

I hear of Barbara Cohen, former Director of News at NPR, probably at an age younger than mine.

A woman with her own fashion line...The CEO of a corporation...the head of a new division at my own organization.

Achievement.

Or there's my old friend, with three daughters, at home in a beautiful domestic setting, her home like an art form.

Women who hire out as expensive consultants and have children at home.

I wonder why I have not achieved more. At worst, I think first that I lack beauty and goals; at best, these qualities are poorly defined in me.

Living in a rented three-bedroom apartment (after a national and NYC financial collapse led us to lose ownership of our co-op apartment in Brooklyn) and a lack of motivation to change that. A closet I've been "meaning to clean out" for six months, clothes that need mending, a piano that needs playing, paintings that need painting, books that need reading, computer software that needs learning, children that have an unquenchable thirst for attention.

The fact is, if that thirst is quenched, the kids create their own activities and space. So I know, my procrastination is not because of them.

Today I thought I want to be an editor, teach at the university level, write, produce...but also to "do work that needs to be done."

So, what needs to be done? What can I contribute?

When I first heard of the Bahai faith, it struck me as true to myself. And what do I want my children to "believe?" What assumptions do I want them to make? Assumptions that are inclusive, not exclusive; a pro-active effort to join hands, to understand.

The consumer movement is not mission enough to my way of thinking, even when the goal is "universal health care." I need something more universal than that.

I say: I love you, Dad. I will miss you. I have missed you for quite a few years. Your spirit suffered so near the end.

Dad says: Take the leap of faith and work will take its place as a means to food, clothing, shelter. As far as work goes, make efforts toward a better life for all. Keep writing. A book will come of it. Maybe more than one. You will have the financial security when the time comes for you to do it. And you will have earned it yourself. No one can take that achievement from you.

Song of the Worker

July 27, 1992

I want to
Enjoy my work
Respect and trust my fellow workers

I want to
Express myself
Maintain my self-esteem

I want to
Plant a garden of ideas
That can grow and thrive

I want to
See the forest
As well as the trees

I want to
Look forward
To the rest of my life

I want to enjoy my work.

Humanity and Nature

April 8, 1993

I

Buried in the dust
Of history and regrets
I smother from inhaling
My own ashes
The stench of death surrounds me
Like the smell of streets
In lower Manhattan.
I come to hate the city's people
Longing for pastoral scenes,
The shimmering of snow-covered trees
On a moonlit hill in the distance.
The distance itself.

II

Relentless work,
The papers move from one corner of the desk
To another, to a file drawer,
The communications pass into the ether,
Flung toward man and God
In purposeful blasphemy
Flung against the nature of beauty
Where manipulation and control
Are cultivated as an art
And enslavement of human spirit
Is called a mission.

III

Sisyphus pushing eternal weight
Gives up
And is crushed by the boulder of time.
From the heap of flesh,
A flower springs
On the wild, wild mountainside,
The thawing snows course down
Droplets gather and tumble
One over another
Into a rushing stream
Feeding a widening river.
Strong waters
Wash remains to the sea
Where they feed the fish.

IV

A new baby is born
And cliches ring
Truer than truth.

Innocence

1993

Cloud clumps spread across the sky
In signal-like fashion
Casting shadows in ghostly shapes
Over the prairie below.

Not as sentient beings
Yet their very randomness
Conveys a message, encrypted
In molecular structure,

As if they were soldiers
Of different sizes and shapes, marching,
Or battalions of ships sailing to war
In coded formations the enemy could never break.

Across a continent, across a world
Foreign forces may falsely assume
The meaning of these clouds, believing
They will gather to sweep them to an early death.

But these clouds are graceful swans
With no goal but to move gently, peacefully
Through space and time in the color
Of a late summer haze above the earth.

The Endless Dream Stream of Laundry
and the Luxury of Solitude

July 6, 1993

Chapter 1

It all begins as it ends
The bowels uncontrolled
The inconsolable weeping

Shots ring out in a dream
A spray of gunfire
And the President is cut down
And, despite the bitterness,
Tears of shame and powerlessness pour out.

And now, in this fax-frenetic* phase,
I will move the mountain
But you must dig the ditch
My graying temples and arthritic back
Cry out for relief
But God replies only
"This is the way of life."

The twists and turns of a spine
Make knots of nerves in the heart
It is the way of life
It begins as it ends.

Chapter 2

Hey, they are allowed to mix together
Feathers and mechanized knives
And a Van de Graaff generator
And put it on display at the Guggenheim.

So why shouldn't I be here,
A broadcast-fax* talk-radio queen
Ready to rap
To an audience made for poetry.

Making my own tradition
The time-honored blended with novelty
What will poets pay for access?
What will radio pay for voices?
The artist asks
Who will pay me to play?

Chapter 3

In this dream
I meet President Clinton
He asks my advice
I say,
"God knows, if we can't handle this food thing,
We'll never get anywhere with health care."

Chapter 4

Again in dreams
I try to find my way around
An all-women's college campus
Suddenly I realize
They all have homemade clothes
I think, "I can't compete,
I don't sew. And I can't afford
To buy them."
I seek a way out
But find myself trapped in a stairwell corner
With a crumbling railing
And if I try to pull my way up,
I sense the whole building will collapse.
I retreat
Into therapy.

* Fax and "broadcast fax" were pervasive new technologies that sped up communication during this period.

The Need for Fundamental Health Reform & Poetry, Or Lessons from Lorena Bobbitt

Feb. 2, 1994

What is lasting about a crisis
Is the fissures in the earth
Clarity of vision, gnawing pain that won't recede
Past a line drawn in the sands of time.

A woman beaten by her husband
Chops off his most private part
He brags about surgical recovery on cable TV
She's sentenced to psychiatric care.

It is written, we must cut to barest bones
To see what is wrong, what is right
She tried to edit a bad paragraph
Out of the text of her life.

We are left to navigate
The seas of truth
Not only to drive
The information highway.

We must surf and sail
Waters and winds of meaning
That roar beyond the pounding
Of electronic pavement.

Childhood Then and Now

Feb. 17, 1994

I am four or five years old on a warm summer day with an easy breeze brushing through my hair. Clusters of perfectly round concord grapes hang heavy from the unpruned vines above me. A cloud of white dust is on them even though no pesticides have been used in the yard. I lay on my back, looking up at the thick-skinned fruit and reach out my tiny hand that looks gigantic to me as I pull a grape off the bunch. I plunge it into my mouth. It is sweet with a deep purple cover; the next is half green and so sour. I pucker, then swallow hard, searching for another sweet as the first.

In later years, our entire back yard is like this second grape. After years of wondrous discovery there, I look across and see it, seemingly, for what it is – just grass and flowers and trees and weeds, a tired old brown garage to the side. It's lost its luster. I've passed some benchmark in time, lost some innocence, closed off a small part of my mind.

This happened again this year. At age 41, I said to myself, the purpose of work is solely income, benefits, security – not adventure, excitement, fulfillment. Work is an obligation to meet, not a life to express. And I wonder, is this a permanent change and a closing forever to wonder through work? Or just a temporary phase that arises with middle-aged growing pains, a tension soon to loosen and flow with the juices of a deeper passion that I'm around the corner from discovering?

It is a more fundamental question than that between the roles of a journalist or that of an information officer. It is an approach to living, a response to circumstance, a putting of things into perspective.

Little can compare to the thrill and joy of seeing your children develop, thrive, and grow. My job performance appraisal, while quite good, matters far less than my son's amazing report card or my daughter's charming drawings of a brown bear she has named Bear-ry.

Gratitude

1994

Susan, Lelia, Lena, Elspeth, Nicole, Pat, Sue, Linda, Kerry, Connie, Patti, Johanna, Kelli, Janet, Maria, Regina, Lisa, Anne, Barbara, Karen, and more whose names I am ashamed to say I can't recall.

These are the women, and even a few men, who have helped us raise our kids. They came in all shapes and size, colors, religions, and ages. They have given my babies hugs and kisses, pats on the back, words of encouragement, and rules to follow. Michelle from Bright Horizons used her long, beautifully manicured fingernail to get a pea out of my daughter's nose. Pat held my son's head at the emergency room when his chin was sliced open on the corner of the afterschool playhouse.

These caregivers work 10-hour days for salaries below $20,000 per year in metro Chicago and New York, preparing my children and thousands of others for the trials of life that lay ahead. They care for our most precious national asset. Why can't we do better by them?

The Color of Memory

October 1994

Race walking down an aqueduct path
The setting sun blazing behind billowy clouds
Throwing white light through autumn branches
Reds, yellows, magentas, and burnt oranges
Soothe optic nerves weary from the week at a computer screen

Colors excite cones of memories
Of past joys learning in a new school year
The annual visit to the family farm
When the orchards yield for harvest
Under Uncle Floyd's and Aunt Eula's gracious care

All reminding me
Dad has died
The family farm is sold
I am severed forever
From the crisp, clean, sweet yet tangy taste
Of a Wagner Macintosh apple.

Building the Vocal Majority

1995 Unpublished Essay

In recent months, I've exercised my personal freedom of speech anonymously in chat groups on the Internet.

This was not always the case. In 1969 and '70, I was a teenaged anti-Vietnam war protester in an Air Force town. It took courage to speak out and be clearly identified, along with a handful of other pariahs, in my conservative Catholic and military community. To my once-beloved parents, I had become one of the "bums" that President Nixon blamed for ruining the American dreams of prosperity, law, and order.

But a greater law and order was at stake – a moral order outlined by St. Augustine, who had developed a strong theory of just war. After learning about it in Christian Doctrine class at school, I firmly believed that my government, whether its leaders were Democrat or Republican, had violated the sacred precepts of this theory. What seemed worse, my Church did not strongly condemn this injustice against humanity in accordance with its teaching. By the age of 16, I felt robbed of my faith in human institutions of authority. My conscience called me to speak out, but as a naïve high school student, I "acted out," and suffered the consequences.

Last night, as I watched a documentary about Richard Nixon, I recalled nightmares I had after we learned Cambodia had been bombed—my sleep disturbed by the total blackout of news access, by earlier images of napalmed Vietnamese children with peeling skin, by steady streams of body bags holding young American men, and by the terror of nuclear confrontation with the USSR. Later, at the time of the Nixon impeachment hearings, I felt that he had been let off the hook for his greatest crimes – those of misleading the American public for four more years in an immoral war he could have ended swiftly and with dignity in 1969, if truth rather than power had been his guiding force.

Now, at the age of 43, I can clearly see how my deepest feelings and many of my concepts about American politics and government were shaped in the decade between 1963 and 1973, from the time I was 11 until 21. These formative years were plagued by such national dramas as:

- Assassinations and funerals of a President, a Presidential candidate, peaceful civil rights leaders, and student anti-war protesters;

- A war that made no moral or military sense;

- Abuses of power by a President, an FBI Director, and courts of law;

- Civil upheaval and violence with such frequent video of police brutality on national TV that Rodney King seems like a faint, distant echo;

- A burgeoning drug trade and frequently corrupt law enforcement that allowed organized crime to control the ghettos and stretch into middle-class suburbs.

Tested today by the responsibilities of parenthood, marriage, a household, a professional job, and building and maintenance of a local community, I continuously search for the moral compass I've had to forge outside institutions. In today's political climate, I am reaching for the voice of courage in which I once spoke about the nation and world. But I choke and struggle for words and convictions.

There is no one stifling my dissent now. I only have to say what I believe. To that end, I thank God for the restoration of faith that has come from memories, history, and experience outside the years 1963 to 1973.

I believe in government that is accountable to the people. And I believe the freshmen Republicans who want to tear it down now represent, despite their twisted rhetoric, forces like those that destroyed my faith during those crucial years of American history. The current House and Senate leadership should be ashamed for catering to such destructive impulses. Congressional representatives who have abandoned positions of leadership should be censured for turning their backs on a fight that must be fought.

A third party and an election will not come soon enough. We must hold elected officials, at every level, accountable **now**, as they shape policy that affects our lives.

We are the people who overcame slavery, set limits on robber barons, brought fascism to its knees, built a world-class economy, and sent images of our fragile planet spinning in space to the world. I have never lost faith in the American people. Help me keep this faith and make our voices loud and clear.

Working Mom Vs. Career Only Woman

1998

My days were packed with wrenched heartstrings
When dropping off my toddlers
To daycare providers at industrial parks
In manicured suburban American landscapes
While you met famous sultans
And suffering swallows in faraway
Mideastern Kingdoms

But it was imprinted in the very marrow
Of my DNA
That I would sit here
Cat in lap, book at bay, pen in hand
While you were destined to wander,
Searching for love and floral anecdotes
Across the globe
And become the author
That I only dream of dabbling as.

My pain is deep and searing
Buried yet impossible to hide
My passions have been tied up with mouths stuffed
But I have this real, true family
A center
I know who and what I am
As modest as that is

Joy is the smile on my child's face
Peace is the calm breathing
Of my amber dog
On a weeknight of a busy work week
In a very mundane life.

1990 - Linda with her mother, Eleanor, at the nursing home in the first year after her mother's strokes. Eleanor's right side was paralyzed, and she had severe aphasia. Eleanor lived at the nursing home until the spring of 2005, a total of nearly 16 years.

Linda on a hike in Autumn 1998 with her family, one of their favorite outdoor activities together.

DECADE IV: 2000 - 2009

Midlife Crises: Age 48-57

Facing Islamic Fundamentalism, Living Online, Crashing Markets, the First Black American President of the USA and Massive Personal Change

I was surprised and disappointed that, among my voluminous files, notebooks, and journals from the past 50 years, I found only one piece of personal writing during the years between 2000 and 2007. One reason is that I often wrote on a computer then, and I no longer have access to files from that laptop because its hard drive crashed.

A larger reason, upon looking back, is what was happening in my personal and professional life in those years. I cannot imagine I had time for poetry, or for essays that weren't part of my job.

As the decade started, our son was 14, our daughter was 11, and both were in middle school. My husband, a criminal prosecutor in NYC, had been elected to our local School Board in mid-1999, after a middle school teacher, too drunk to drive after a New Year's Eve party, was caught by parents in their home committing an act of pedophilia upon their young son. For three years, our family was directly involved in dozens of heated school board meetings that resulted in the firing of the teacher and two aides, the resignation of two principals and a superintendent, and the hiring of their replacements.

Nothing fires up a community like the issues in a school district. I discovered more than I ever cared to know about the attitudes of many parents toward the education and discipline of their children and intricacies of the lives of their families. Volunteer service for a school board or PTSA is a noble commitment and sacrifice. But you need to have - or develop - very thick skin to maintain an even-keeled temperament. These days you may even find that you need extra security for you and your family. And while it's extremely rare, there are some teachers or coaches who, disliking your involvement in a Board or PTSA decision, will take their frustration out on your children. School board participation has grown even more tense in the twenty-first century as some parents have grown eager to ban books or teaching materials, even some that have been valued by teachers and students for decades.

In my work life in early 2000 as the Communications/Media lead on Consumers Union's litigation team, I collaborated for our side with a team of high-powered, take-no-prisoners attorneys in California. I had to be present for weeks at the organization's first-ever jury trial in Los Angeles (Isuzu v. CU), working from six a.m. to nine p.m. to meet East Coast and West Coast media deadlines, while simultaneously managing a media relations team in Yonkers, NY. CU won the case, and despite a light slap on the wrist by the jury, CU achieved an overall victory in the court of public opinion.

When I was first hired into Consumers Union/Consumer Reports in 1990, a woman attorney named Rhoda Karpatkin was the organization's CEO. When she retired in December 2000, the male Board Chairman took over as CEO in January 2001. I was told by many colleagues that I had been quietly labeled as a "holdover" from the previous regime; in early 2001, a female consultant warned me that my days at CU would likely be numbered, even though I had a seat on the executive team. Within a couple of years, many women managers from various departments came to me and quietly complained about changes in the workplace climate that were adversely affecting them. This work environment hung over me like a dark storm cloud for several years.

Another major shift occurred in late 2000, after eight years of Democrat Bill Clinton's Presidency. Given the electoral college system in the U.S., the vote for a new President came down to a contest over disputed ballots in the state of Florida. Vice President Al Gore was the Democratic Party's

Presidential candidate; Gore had promised to prioritize his Climate Change Action Plan, an increase in the minimum wage, and a more generous family leave policy among his other goals. But the U.S. Supreme Court heard the now infamous "hanging chad" Florida vote count case. Even though Gore had won the popular vote by more than a half million ballots, and the electoral college outcome depended on the disputed Florida vote count, five out of nine Supreme Court Justices determined that Republican George W. Bush would be the next President of the USA. George W. took office on January 20, 2001.

Just nine months later, on September 11, 2001, I.S.I.S. terrorists took control of four planes and crashed them into the World Trade Center Twin Towers in NYC, the Pentagon, and a field in Pennsylvania. For weeks, the news media – and I – became obsessed with learning all we could about how and why such evil acts could be undertaken by anyone. The event had a profound impact on all of us, including our young daughter, who developed acute anxiety that morphed into panic attacks during the following year. Her mental health became a priority for me, as did our son's newly expressed desire to join the military or apply to West Point.

The only benefits I saw come from 9/11 were the short-lived unity of the American people and the empathy across the world for our suffering this terrorist attack. Within months, travel agents were urging Americans to overcome their newly developed fear of flying. In February 2002, our family took advantage of a terrifically affordable offer of airfare and hotel in Florence, Italy. We stayed for about one week, with side trips to Assisi and Rome. Our presence, and of course, our American money were welcomed with open arms. But we also experienced a genuine feeling of consolation from the Italians and other Europeans we met, all of whom expressed shock at the traumatic events of 9/11.

For our family, the trip was a dream-come-true escape into Renaissance history that both our children had been studying recently. We shared the wonder at the artistic and architectural beauty of Florence, along with its robust cuisine. Our young teens were thrilled when offered wine at restaurants.

We walked throughout the city, taking in all the sights we could fit into our timeframe. We bought beautifully crafted leather shoes and jackets and other smaller mementos. We struggled to speak Italian, but it was rarely needed. Most of all, the vacation gave us a deeply needed sense of historic continuity and the meaning of America to others in the world.

Getting back to my work routine after these travels in 2002, I learned that a separate six-year legal battle between my employer, Consumers Union, and the Suzuki Motor Corporation had wound its way through the federal court system. In 2004, after a trial date was finally set, the two parties agreed to an out-of-court settlement. But another corporation, Sharper Image, slapped CU with another lawsuit. That case ended in late 2004, with the company ordered to pay CU's legal fees. I had spent more than eight hard years successfully defending the advocate Consumers Union/Consumer Reports against corporate lawsuits in the court of public opinion, while leading a team that kept a positive view of the organization, its publications, and its integrity before the news media and public.

In January 2005, I had lunch with my colleague Elizabeth Crow, then Consumer Reports' Editorial Director. Elizabeth could celebrate tremendous accomplishments in the publishing world and a leadership style appreciated by her direct reports. But a male executive colleague had referred to her in my presence as "an empty suit." The following month, at an executive leadership retreat that I attended, one of the male V.P.s brought up "gender issues." Soon after that retreat, I sat behind that same V.P. in a large staff meeting while he suffered a heart attack at age 50. A couple months later, in early April, I learned that Elizabeth, age 58, had just died from esophageal cancer. At age 53 myself, I began thinking seriously about the impact that my work environment was having on my own health and habits.

Just one week after Elizabeth's death, while attending an executive meeting, I was interrupted by my assistant to take a call from the nursing home where my mother had spent the previous 17 years, half paralyzed from hemorrhagic strokes. A nurse told me it was time to say goodbye to my mother.

I returned to the executive meeting to explain the family emergency and be on my way. While the CEO continued a long monologue to the assembled group, he ignored me standing next to him. When I was finally allowed to explain the situation, I saw only annoyance in the CEO's face and demeanor. Such an apparent lack of empathy at that moment is difficult to forget.

I left that day to join my siblings at the nursing home in central NYS, and on April 18, 2005, my mother died. Standing in her room at the nursing home after we emptied the shelves, closet, dresser and walls, the finality of the loss hit me hard even though she had suffered a long, slow decline. I was grateful to have my siblings nearby to share stories, songs, and recollections of our days and years with our mother. I was comforted by my husband, children, and old friends who joined us for the wake and funeral. Dozens of colleagues (even the CEO) sent condolence cards.

Few events cause you to contemplate your life and health more than the death of your mother. On the advice of several female colleagues, I hired a labor lawyer to help me address my concerns about my work environment; over several months, she negotiated a package for me. In September 2005, I started an Executive MPA program at Columbia University. In early November, I strapped on my golden parachute and gladly took the leap out of CU.

About six weeks later, I suffered an acute gall stone attack and spent hours in a hospital emergency room in pain until a nurse bent down to whisper in my ear, "Take the morphine!" I was scheduled for surgery in January. A couple weeks before my operation, my daughter contracted a severe case of mono that left her bedridden for more than a month in the middle of her junior year in high school. I am forever grateful that my sister Diane kindly traveled to our home to help both of us during our recovery.

In April 2006, I started a new full-time media relations position at Associated Press at their world headquarters in Manhattan while continuing the MPA program at Columbia. The job was a pressure-cooker, responding to online attacks by right-wing media critics while undertaking projects to boost

AP's positive public profile. In my first few months, I had to manage public and media relations surrounding an employee's suicide threat, the detainment by the U.S. military of an AP photographer accused of terrorist sympathies, social media disinformation by extremists who attacked the journalistic integrity of the Associated Press, and numerous other hostile situations.

My most enjoyable assignment was conducting video interviews with AP photographers who had shot some of the most iconic images of 9/11 about that experience and its impact on them, after they had returned to the same sites five years later to capture new images of NYC's remarkable recovery. The photos and video interviews became part of a traveling exhibit that I helped to produce and book at sites around the U.S. Despite the many positives about the job and many of my colleagues, some other aspects of the working conditions at AP led me to resign after one year.

I moved on in April 2007 to a much kinder, gentler position at a long-term care center in the Bronx, where I negotiated a four-day work week to compensate for a lower salary. Working as an executive within the music therapy group at this health facility, I was better able to see my daughter through her last semester of high school and continue my MPA program at Columbia University.

By mid-2007, my husband and I were considering the changes that an empty nest might bring. Meanwhile, my economics courses were making me acutely aware that serious trouble was brewing in the economy. I could see that, given our usual monthly expenses plus the pending cost of college for our daughter, our income and assets would not equip us for a market collapse. After our daughter's high school graduation that June, and about one year before the 2008 crash and subsequent Great Recession, we sold our home and moved to a nearby rental home.

Our daughter left for college in Montreal, Canada in September 2007. Despite high grades, she had a rough time at McGill University, and we urged her to drop out after her first year there. She came home in May 2008 and stayed with us until she started courses at a nearby college for the arts, where she thrived. Also, that May, I finished my MPA, and our son graduated from the University of Chicago with a degree in Economics. Given the shakiness of the economy and his long-held dream of playing professional baseball, he tried out for a non-affiliated minor league team and was accepted onto a team in Nevada as a left-handed pitcher. He was off on his own that summer, and by late 2008, our daughter had settled happily into her new school.

While all this was happening, Barry and I had been exploring possibilities for buying a new home in Westchester County. Weighing the costs of real estate and high property taxes there against our ages and income, our financial adviser suggested that we move to a less expensive region. Barry was recruited to and began a position in early 2008 in Albany, New York as General Counsel for a state commission. He rented a studio apartment in Albany where he stayed during the week while I continued working in the Bronx and finishing my master's degree. For nearly eight months, he commuted on weekends between his rented apartment in Albany and our rented house in Westchester County.

With my MPA in hand that summer, I landed a job in Albany as an Executive Director of a small, statewide nonprofit association for local health officials. We bought a house in Albany, moved there in August 2008, and I began my new position in November.

When you add all of this up, it's not surprising that I found so little time for my own personal writing.

More Thoughts on the 2000 – 2009 Decade

The leadership, news media, and hence, the public in the USA too often ignore major changes in other parts of the world that can dramatically affect our national security. This became crystal clear on September 11, 2001, when the World Trade Center and the Pentagon were targeted and attacked by suicide pilots who were members of I.S.I.S. Despite this revolutionary assault, how many Americans today know that I.S.I.S. stood for Islamic State of Iraq and Syria, that there was an alternative name of I.S.I.L. that stood for

Islamic State of Iraq and the Levant, or that this was a Sunni Muslim group that claimed religious authority over all Muslims, inspired by Al Qaeda but later publicly expelled from it? How many Americans today understand the role that Saudi Arabian leaders played in supporting I.S.I.S.? In 2001, what did Americans know about support that the USA had given in the 1980s to rebel Mujahideen forces that fought the Soviet Union when Russians tried to establish control over Afghanistan?

I was as ignorant in September 2001 as any other American about these matters. I was shocked and baffled by the evil intent of the suicide pilots who intentionally crashed into the World Trade Center and the Pentagon. I had no understanding of the revolutionary fervor and deeply rooted beliefs of fundamentalist Islamic terrorism. And I was horrified when the smell of burning flesh, mingled with the ashes of incinerated skyscrapers, reached my small village north of Manhattan.

Our insulated world was focused on technological advances spurred by the creation of the Internet, which had sprung from the defense establishment of the USA. How ironic that this focus led the USA to take its eyes off forces that rely on the most basic - and base - human powers of violence and hatred, disguised as revolutionary religious righteousness. I.S.I.S. used tools, weapons and vulnerabilities that were handed to them by the USA to attack this nation that they viewed as the worst of the infidels.

By the dawn of the new millennium with 2000, American society, along with most of the world, had fully abandoned the era of industrialization for a data-driven "knowledge economy" and "information age." This economic revolution had gradually shifted economies of the 1970s and 1980s from the production of material goods to the production of "intellectual capital." I doubt that many economists foresaw how this shift in production from goods to data and information would later lead to revolutionary upheavals in social behavior, from adolescent bullying to online buying to addictions to social media and rampant disinformation.

Just as we were oblivious to the full impact of the Internet and new forms of international terrorism, global markets were caught off-guard about the severe penalties that financial industry deregulation would exact from nearly everyone in 2008. Predatory lending in home mortgages, a flood of hedging activity, and a web of sketchy derivatives led to market crashes. Soon, we experienced an overall decline in wealth of 40% or more in all types of assets, and the deepest, longest-lasting global recession since the Great Depression of the late 1920s and 1930s. Personally, I experienced an enormous drop by late 2009 in the value of my Individual Retirement Account (IRA) and of the Albany home we had purchased in August 2008.

On the political scene, a young Democratic Senator Barack Obama was campaigning for President with his V.P. running mate Joe Biden when the markets collapsed. Obama's campaign was already strong due to a dismal performance by President George W. Bush, an unpopular war in Iraq, an already weak economy, and a most unfortunate running mate, Alaska Governor Sarah Palin, chosen by Republican candidate John McCain. The role Republican policies had played in ushering in the disastrous 2008 market collapse helped to seal the fate of Republican candidates in that November's election. Excitement about the historic ascension of the nation's first Black President was palpable. "Yes, We Can," was the message of hope that Obama shouted to a broad spectrum of voters.

At the beginning his Presidency, recovery and regulation renewal and reform were Barack Obama's top priorities, followed closely by health insurance reforms that came to be known as the Affordable Care Act. Republicans who opposed the legislation tried to denigrate it by calling it "Obamacare." But most Americans applauded the broader availability of health coverage and protections from insurance abuses. "Obamacare" has been embraced by the public and the courts over time as a positive development for millions of Americans who would be unable to afford health care without it.

On the personal front, my life between 2000 and 2009 was consumed with trying to meet the needs of love, care, and guidance of pre-teen and teenage children. We were saving whatever we could toward the college education of these two very bright, accomplished students. Throughout the 2000-2009 decade, my husband went through a rocky series of career moves, leading me to feel that the burden of stable income rested on my shoulders.

I was in a well-compensated leadership position at Consumers Union, with increasingly complex and time-consuming demands, especially given the years of work on litigation communications. But the cost to me personally is difficult to measure. The worst was the time lost in being with my family. A mother who works outside the home is highly likely, if not certain, to feel inadequate and riddled with sorrow and guilt about time she might have spent with her children. And yet, we make the choices that seem necessary when considering all the factors.

Despite 15 years of dedication, excellent performance reviews, and personal sacrifice that included the public defense of my employer when it was under attack, it became clear by early 2005 that the CEO of Consumers Union/Consumer Reports wanted his own new communications leader. I had hit a dead end. Many of my working relationships at Consumers Union with bright, dedicated colleagues have blossomed into long-term friendships that I still value deeply. Unfortunately, that CEO is not among them. When I left the organization, my departure had the emotional hallmarks of a bitter divorce from a demeaning relationship.

Tough times like these are complicated further when you are in the "sandwich generation" between growing children and declining parents. When my mother died at the nursing home after living there for 17 years, I became a parent orphaned by my own parents. Soon, my children would leave me and my husband with an empty nest. When this happens, you feel a tectonic shift in your perspective on life.

By late 2008, I had no children at home, I had completed my master's degree, and I had newfound leisure time. And so, in addition to my new job and settling into a new home, I finally started writing and researching a memoir that had haunted me for decades. Focused on my early years and several traumas I experienced between 1952 and early 1973, I self-published the manuscript through TBM Books and Book Baby with financial and emotional support from family, old friends, and many former colleagues. Titled *"Unearthing the Ghosts: A Mystery Memoir,"* its core story is summarized in this current book at the beginning of Section I, under the title, "The Research Psychiatrist's Subject."

Other than one unpublished essay below, found in a hard copy, my previous book must represent my personal writing during this 2000-2009 decade.

What Went Wrong in the 1990s Health Care Debate?

Decade IV - Written in 2000

Everyone framed the question. The simple answer, from the standpoint of consumers, is that Congress and the President couldn't get it together. There was a failure of political will. The parties couldn't put partisanship aside. They paid too much attention to the special interest lobbies and their money. The people were way ahead of the politicians. The politicians had no courage.

The other common parlance is that Clinton gave away the store before anyone came in to demand anything. He negotiated it all away before the debate began. A failure of personality. He's too wishy washy for the job. Perhaps his wife is too arrogant for hers.

The single payer proponents like us feared the fight was all over when Clinton announced, before the election, that he favored "managed competition." That announcement may have helped to get him the endorsement of *The New York Times*, which may have helped elect him as President. But it doomed his plan to complexity, even while he spouted rhetoric about simplicity.

Then, of course, there is the invective of the Republicans and the right wing. Win at any price. Capitalistic ideology above pragmatism, above the public good.

These voices had the power of negativism on their side. The power of a cynical public mood, and an uncertain economy (even while it turned around and grew). People do not feel settled about their jobs. They don't want to see jobs lost. People are afraid of being without health care coverage, but they are more afraid of losing their jobs. The small business lobby played this fear to the hilt.

There are the hard, cold facts about what it takes to get a piece of national legislation of any type passed these days. Clinton and other universal health care advocates tried to play their hand through the news media, national and local. All the time, the small business lobby was building an onerous machine that can spit out thousands of phone calls and letters to members of Congress at the touch of a few (figurative) buttons. Their machine was finely tuned, well-greased. Ours was still in the process of being built. And liberal political activists got caught up in 1960s nostalgia for national bus tours and rallies instead of 1990s realities of telemarketing and phone and fax banks.

The fact is, the opponents of reform were far better educated about the techniques of political persuasion in the age of a hundred channels on cable TV, and a thousand right-wing radio talk show hosts across the U.S. radio spectrum. Those hosts were in daily touch with keeping a wild and wooly audience entertained.

While liberals and progressives were in awe of the ability to talk to each other and themselves through computer interconnections, the conservatives and reactionaries were using new techniques to reach mass audiences and move them to action, like promising them that, with one, short, free 800-number call, they could deliver their opposition messages to all their representatives and Senators in one fell swoop.

In short, the various business lobbies dealt with this issue as if it were business survival warfare. We dealt with it as if it was a campaign for the public good. I hate to say it, but guess who defined the terms of battle?

We failed to identify cost containment for the individual consumer household as the primary motivator. Universal coverage was the wrong principle to put first. Middle class families are worried about their own financial security. We failed to demonstrate in dollars and cents how universal coverage helps protect their financial security.

It's also arguable that Consumers Union (CU) was intellectually disingenuous. One major reason we undertook this campaign was because of the impact of rising health care coverage costs on the business of doing business at CU. That should have been up front.

We didn't really want an employer mandate; we wanted it taken off our plate of benefits altogether. We could have made a very compelling case for single payer from an employer's perspective, as well as from a consumer perspective. In fact, employers are the primary consumers of health insurance in this country. Somehow, we weren't bold enough to be direct about this fact. We could have been a leader of employers/consumers while protecting the interests of individual consumer households. Instead, we shied away from the truth.

Too little time, effort, and money was focused on clarifying the economic impact of health care reform on consumers – both employers/consumers and individual families. We had policy analysis of the various proposals instead of a real down-to-earth "shopper's guide."

We could blame the media, but the fact is the media is entirely caught up in its own crises. The convergence of media, the fragmentation of the audiences, the introduction of C-Span – all these factors and more that are part of the sweeping changes in the communications industry— have discouraged the kind of powerful network television coverage that might have been comparable to what you'd see in a political campaign. The issue was virtually ignored by network TV news departments that were too busy trying to launch the latest evening magazine show in a ratings race with their competitors.

Last, but not least, we are a nation with an individualistic ethic that has grown so strong, overbearing, and dominating, it threatens every potential avenue of community. The right to bear arms outstrips the need to protect children. Why should it be so surprising that universal health coverage is so difficult to achieve in this atmosphere? There is virtually no consensus on the most basic concepts of healing.

This debate could have been – God willing, it can still become – a source of healing for this nation. A way to focus our vision on the need for community in our lives, for a social contract with each other through good government. At this point in time, it has torn us further asunder.

Who will really show us the error of our ways?

Linda at a 2004 Consumer Reports/Consumers Union Senior Leadership Team retreat.

Linda and her family at her daughter Joanna's high school graduation
in 2007, along the Hudson River in Dobbs Ferry, NY.

DECADE V PLUS: 2010 - 2022

Back to the Future: Age 58-70

Death Bells Toll; A Call to Collective Healing

I began the 21st century's second decade at the age of 58, a post-menopausal woman whose parents had passed away and whose children had moved on with their adult lives. These years cover a little more than a decade, and they've been packed with far more than an entire lifetime should be. To begin, between 2010 and 2020, eight members of my family died. They were my father-in-law Sam, mother-in-law Helen, the spouses (Bill, Charlie, John, Jim, and Jeanne) of my five older siblings, and the 16-year-old son Nate of my nephew Rich. Then, a sweeping pandemic took the lives of at least an additional one million Americans and 15 million worldwide, including relatives (mother, husband, wife) of friends. In 2020 alone, seven people whom I knew passed away – some who tested COVID positive, some whose demise may have been related indirectly to the pandemic.

Thankfully, this decade-plus of death was counterbalanced between 2015 – 2022 by the births of five beautiful grandchildren, the "Littles" who give us a clear reason to hope and work for a better future world. I believe this work is not only for my own kids and grandkids, but for all children in our human family.

* * *

Intense drama unfolded on the larger political stage during this period with the sunset of the Obama presidency, defeat of Hillary Clinton, and rise of Trump's MAGA brand of Republicanism. Meanwhile, my life in the workplace, home front, and eventual retirement chugged along. From late 2008 - 2017, I worked as the Executive Director of the NYS Association of County Health Officials (NYSACHO), taking knowledge gained from reporting, nonprofit leadership, and communication about public health topics to a new level. It became my last full-time professional job before semi-retirement and then full retirement. NYSACHO gave me many valuable new experiences as a nonprofit collaborator with state and local government officials, a lobbyist for public health resources, and an educator about public health risks and rewards. I had a small but terrific organizational team, and a group of extremely dedicated members and Board members. Unfortunately, I walked into this position at a difficult time for obtaining public health funding, due largely to the long tail of the 2008 financial collapse.

While facing funding struggles, my NYSACHO work life focused on community disease prevention and health promotion – from education about immunization against infectious disease and the health dangers of eating and drinking too much sugar, to the community health risks reported in states that allowed extensive hydrofracking for gas and oil. Between 2009 and 2017, Public Health Emergency Preparedness focused on everything from bioterrorism risks and climate change threats to containing potential pandemics from viruses that caused H1N1 influenza in 2009, MERS in 2012, and Ebola between 2013 – 2016.

Although tensions are typical between layers of government, my organization's members who led county health departments usually collaborated well with their partners in big city, state, and federal agencies and with healthcare practitioners in medical offices and hospitals, all with the goal of improving the health of the population in their communities and improving the performance of all involved in guarding population health. Emergency preparedness and environmental health experts began focusing on the mitigation of climate change impacts that scientists knew would arrive with increasing intensity. A significant increase in powerful storms led to flooding in New York City and upstate New York areas that existing infrastructure and human resources were unable to handle. Throughout the U.S. and world, a new trend of searing summer heat and drought led to numerous electrical grid failures, wildfires, and a desperate need for emergency cooling centers to protect lives and health.

At the end of 2017, I retired from NYSACHO and began a two-year period of part-time consulting, working for nonprofit causes that I valued. The last was the New York Coalition of Community Development Financial Institutions (CDFIs). This organization and its members help improve the social determinants of health by improving the financial health of communities. They provide low-interest loans and financial education to individuals, small business owners, and organizations that serve marginalized populations and poverty-stricken geographic areas and have difficulty obtaining financing from more traditional lenders. For one year, I helped the group expand its membership and build an online infrastructure.

By late 2018, family-care demands emerged due to the welcome arrival of grandchildren, the fear of vision loss for my husband, and a health crisis when my eldest sister suffered a bad fall. I sought a personal financial plan from an advisor to determine whether full retirement for both me and my husband would be feasible. After assurance that we had the resources to live in relative comfort through our later years, Barry and I ceased any aggressive marketing for consulting work, while considering any options that might arise. As it happened, we made the move in December 2019, just before the world learned of the SARS-COV2/COVID pandemic.

As I write this, that pandemic is ongoing, and its impacts are fresh in my mind. But it coincided with my full retirement from the workforce, and I find it difficult to parse out which personal changes flowed from retirement versus pandemic restriction. To trace those changes, I need to wander back in greater detail through my evolutions between 2010-2022, changes that occurred outside the work world and beyond the larger political environment.

The loss of my husband's parents, Sam in 2010 and Helen in 2011, was the first big hit. When Sam and Helen first met me in 1973, they barely welcomed me into their Jewish home. As his mother said within earshot of Barry's younger brother, "It's not so bad she's not Jewish, but Catholic?" However, as we came to know each other through the years, we came to love and value each other as family. All the members of both families joined together in joy, laughter, and dance at our festive wedding in November 1979. Most important, after our children were born, Sam and Helen were wonderful grandparents to them.

The end of their lives was painful for all in the family. The physical distance of Barry and his siblings from their parents in their final days and hours made their passing even more traumatic. After their mother's death, they went through a long period of emotional upheaval. My children and one of my nephews on the Wagner side attended the funeral services and sat shiva, as is done in the Jewish tradition. I experienced the Jewish prayers, El Maleh Rahamim and the Mourner's Kaddish in a deeper sense than ever before.

Supporting a spouse through the death of their parents is one of the most sacred fulfillments of marriage vows. When we marry another person, we marry into another family whose emotions and practices are wrapped in history long before our spouse began their life with us.

Grandpa Sam's death in 2010 was a watershed moment for our son also. He had left his Illinois baseball team mid-season to attend the funeral in Florida. While walking along the beach at dusk after the services, he received a call from his coach releasing him from the team, apparently because he had put his family above his sport. When he returned to Illinois, they called him back to pitch, and for the first time during his three summers of pro baseball, he said, "No thanks." The connection to family he experienced after the death of his grandfather signaled the end of his minor league baseball career and the start of his search for a life partner. He moved to San Francisco with his girlfriend at that time and worked as an auto mechanic, furthering him along a path toward engineering. After he was accepted with a scholarship into the Mechanical Engineering program at North Carolina State University, he moved to Raleigh.

Our daughter, still in art school, had a boyfriend at that time whose parents seemed convinced that they would eventually marry. But in the Fall of 2011, after Helen died, Joanna began questioning her commitment to that young man. By the time she finished with her BFA in May 2012, she had a new beau in her sights, and this young man, Jack, clearly had her in his heart. When she took a job at a woodworking shop in Philadelphia, Jack found a job at a nearby Apple store, determined to follow her along her future path.

In the meantime, Barry, in his position with a NY State Ethics commission, encountered major political and governmental shifts after Governor Elliot Spitzer resigned in the midst of a prostitution scandal. This shock was followed by a more minor ethics violation by Spitzer's successor, and the swearing in of a new Governor, Andrew Cuomo, at the end of 2010. By the end of Cuomo's first year in office in 2011, Barry began a new executive position in risk management at another NY State agency. Once he had settled into this new role, our lives settled into a routine in Albany, with occasional visits to and from our adult children.

Earlier that year, in July 2011, another family death hit me hard. Bill, the spouse of my eldest sister Joan, died at age 71 after his year-long battle with a pre cancerous cyst led to pancreatic and liver cancer that metastasized further. Given our geographic proximity, my relationships with their grown children, and most disturbing to me, the fact that Bill's death was the first in my generation in our family, mortality stared coldly at me. The death of Barry's mother just two months later intensified that stare. And in 2012, Barry and I turned 60 years old. We began to think about our "end games."

By mid-2012, our children were grown, employed and healthy, even if they were still working on even healthier psyches (as were we). We had begun settling into a later phase of our lives, with an eye toward retirement and beyond. In a new community, we struggled to develop new friendships in our senior years. We were very fortunate to have a burgeoning friendship with one couple who introduced us to many others, and who told me about the Woman's Club of Albany, where I met many interesting women.

For a period, we desperately missed our lives as active parents in our former stomping grounds in New York City and Westchester County; we missed our many colleagues and neighbors who had become friends to us and our children.

But gradually, we came to see and appreciate the many assets of Albany and the surrounding region - its proximity to mountain-hiking and canoeing in the Catskills, Berkshires, Adirondacks, and Helderbergs; its many small lakes for summer boating and swimming; numerous well-groomed "rail trails" for bicycling and walking; plentiful venues with great sound acoustics for all the types of live music performance we love; a broad selection of good ethnic and farm-to-table restaurants – and all of this is within a relatively short driving distance, with very affordable prices. If we craved an infusion of Big City life, NYC was just a three-hour train or car ride away; add another 45 minutes and you could be at the ocean.

The only downside to the area was – and still is – that our grown kids had no attachment to it beyond the two of us, and what's worse, the area had no real appeal to them as a place to settle down eventually. Over time, it has become clear that, to see them, we need to travel to wherever they are at least as often as they travel to us.

* * *

How did the larger political landscape look during these years? For me and many others, this period marked the end of hopes wrapped in Barack Obama's presidency and ushered in horrors embedded in Donald Trump's presidency. A revolution crept up on us, and then beat us over the head; it was one in which I wanted no part. At its most extreme, it was a self-righteous, white supremacist, ultra-right revolution, strategized for years by a collection of right-wing think tanks and brought to a fever pitch by one of New York City's most infamous and narcissistic con men, Donald Trump. Trump became the leader and icon of a revolution with fascist overtones, built upon the conservative Tea Party wing of the Republican Party that was founded in 2009. Based upon close observations of Donald Trump's public discourse and persona, a large group of leading psychologists and psychiatrists took the unusual, and, some thought "unprofessional" step of diagnosing Donald Trump as a sociopath, plagued with a total lack of empathy, an "unbridled and extreme present hedonism," paranoia, and narcissism, mixed with a habit of pathological lying. (See Citizen

Therapists Against Trumpism, book titled "The Dangerous Case of Donald Trump" and multiple warnings by individual psychologists.)

The more frightening aspect of this right-wing "revolution," better identified as a severe backlash, was that it was supported by somewhere between 30% and 40% of adult Americans. Furthermore, many, if not most, of Trump's followers and allies had an unwavering belief in their absolute right to hold a cache of guns and ammunition, including military-grade automatic weapons and high-volume magazines (and I don't mean reading material). In addition, Trump supporters were fed by many sources of television and online media that created and promoted false narratives, using distortion, half-truths, and outright lies to mislead people, and even to incite hatred and violence.

This ushered in a phase best described by the title of a book I read recently, "When We Cease to Understand the World." I found that too many people – many public figures, many individual citizens, and some foreign voices (some of which were surely Russian "bots") – people who may have been civil if not entirely honest in their past discourse became increasingly deceptive, crass, cruel, and even viciously violent in expressing their beliefs and views. This has become particularly true in online comment forums, especially with regard to Black and brown people, immigrants, gay, transexual and other nonbinary persons, Jews, people with disabilities, anyone who followed the CDC COVID guidelines, and ultimately, anyone who is an admitted Democrat.

Legal rights and established precedents taken for granted for 50 years or more were thrown under the bus by justices and judges appointed by conservative presidents. A huge swath of the political category once labeled "conservative" became radicalized by anti-scientific conspiracy theories and white supremacist ideology unlike anything seen since the rise of Nazism and Fascism in the 1930s and '40s. One of the more sobering aspects of this trend is that it has been global, not just domestic in the U.S. Increasingly, the American right has found an alluring appeal and even made connections to authoritarian strongmen in nations such as Russia, Hungary, North Korea, China, Venezuela and elsewhere.

At first, the liberal or "left" side of the political spectrum in the U.S. reacted to this dramatically rightward shift with shock and disbelief, followed by satire and biting humor. But as the trend picked up steam, laughter from the left shifted to anger and fear about corrupt minority rule, an imminent threat to basic democracy, a failure to accept fact-based reality, and the breakdown of all civility. Even moderate voices within the conservative or Republican sphere – even Trump's own Vice President Pence and conservative Republican election officials in red states - found themselves targeted by the radical right with grotesque verbal and social media attacks and death threats. While some extremists on the left may have hurled epithets at their opponents, these matched neither the violence, intensity, nor volume of the excrement thrown by the extreme right.

Against this background, another revolution – one that held my sympathy - took root in 2013 and blossomed in 2020 with the horrific murder of George Floyd by a Minneapolis police officer. The Black Lives Matter movement sprung from historical lessons of past Civil Rights and Black Power movements, the hard, smart work of thousands of young Black and brown women and men, outreach and coalition-building with allies, and the ability of smart phones to document violent and racist actions by police and paranoid white folks who, far too often, called the police on Black and brown people for no good reason.

Between 2015 and 2020, the political climate in the USA shouted at me in echoes of deep divisions I had experienced in the 1960s and '70s, during the civil rights and anti-war movements of that era. The difference in this recent period is that people with my viewpoint – supporting Black lives and opposing anti-democratic authoritarianism – were in the majority. And yet, for four years or more, we faced a dictatorship of a misled minority. It was as if we were Alice, fallen into a nightmarish Wonderland. This unreality gave birth to a new batch of revolutionary fervor on the left with the creation of numerous new progressive organizations, including Indivisible, Swing Left, and Stacey Abrams's powerful voting rights nonprofit, Fair Fight, among many others.

The 2020 election was held 50 years after I had first gained the right to vote at age 18, 48 years after I first voted for President in 1972. This time, despite the recurrence of deep political divisions in the USA, my Democratic candidate won. But Trump and his die-hard supporters would not accept the choice of the majority of voters and electors. Instead, they backed an insurrection by thousands of violent protestors who tried, for the first time in American history, to overturn the election results by stopping the vote certification by Congress.

Sadly, the public has grown weary of the news of the January 6, 2021, invasion of the nation's Capital. Outrage over the attempt by a radical minority led by a former president to literally overthrow the government of the United States has bubbled up only within pockets of die-hard Democrats and true conservatives who once had a home in the Republican Party before it became a Trumpist MAGA party. In addition, anti-democratic fervor in "red" states has led to legislative and judicial attempts to reject the 2020 presidential vote that was certified by state electors and Congress, curtail voting by likely Democrats, and install election officials willing to throw out legitimate election results to favor radical right candidates. The U.S. Constitution and Bill of Rights have encountered a serious threat to their survival.

Another, perhaps related, set of threats has been brewing simultaneously on the public health stage. By mid-2020, when the SARS-COV2 pandemic hit hard, practices such as vaccination and masking that protect community well-being, accepted for a century as scientifically valid, became scorned by conspiracy theorists as an alleged "abuse of power by elites who seek to take away our freedoms." The obvious daily evidence of climate change fostered by human activities was denied and treated as a hoax. Statements once known as lies were referenced as "alternative facts" by Trump's presidential spokesperson. Trust in journalism morphed into claims of "fake news." Up became down, in became out, and the Uncertainty Principle, originally established for the comprehension of sub-atomic physics, became the new rule for social order, of which little appeared to remain.

Well before the SARS-COV2/COVID pandemic spread after late 2019, the public health workforce had become like canaries in a coal mine, experiencing early indicators of serious hazards and unprecedented challenges to the well-being of their communities. Plagues of morbid obesity, fresh food "deserts," opioid addition, gun violence, and poorly managed mental illness had become rampant across the nation's geographic and demographic borders. When COVID hit, the American population needed good public health soldiers more than ever. But too many politicians, entertainment news anchors, and social media conspiracy theorists turned the public against the science that is the foundation for good public health practice.

We all became victims to a basic distrust of reality itself, propagated by those whose primary motivation is a will to power, where wealth, greed, religion, bullying, and violence are simply tools for the acquisition and preservation of power.

When I retired, I was determined to devote renewed energies to the political sphere. I connected with progressive organizations whose members were overwhelmingly female and/or nonbinary in gender, collaborating with established racial justice groups as the NAACP, the younger Black Lives Matter movement, and voter rights groups such as Stacy Abrams's Fair Fight. I participated as a volunteer in vigorous postcard, letter-writing, texting, phoning, and in-person canvassing campaigns to get out the vote. We focused heavily on conservative and swing states where legitimate voters were being systematically dumped from the voter rolls for no good reason. We grew concerned, with good reason, that easy access to mail-in ballots, early voting, and other mechanisms that increase voter participation were being systematically restricted or eliminated.

I have grown convinced that a form of suicidal ideation is permeating our body politic and that it must be stopped. A collective death wish can be seen in insurrections and the erosion of voting rights, the allowance for nearly anyone to obtain rapid-fire weapons and ammunition of mass murder, the denial of climate change, hostility toward accepting the tragic mistakes and failures in our own American history, and the failures to address the needs of so many mothers and children that lead to high rates of maternal death and unwanted pregnancies. It can be seen in statistics such as gun violence being the top cause of death of American children, the relatively low SARS-COV2 vaccination rate, the percentage of American people who believe bizarre conspiracy theories, and death rates from suicide and overdoses of fentanyl and other drugs.

These are existential threats that face the entire human species today. The historic SARS-COV2/COVID pandemic has continued with frightening variants through the writing of this manuscript. In a bizarre twist, this enormous global health challenge has fallen victim to political divisions, online disinformation, and a disturbing public failure to embrace a collective community-minded response.

Meanwhile, two additional epidemics are wreaking havoc upon increasingly broad portions of the American public – gun violence that is a daily occurrence in city streets and nearly daily mass shootings that often feature the use of semi-automatic weapons and high-capacity magazines of ammunition, and opioid addiction, often resulting in overdoses of fentanyl, heroin, or prescription drugs such as oxycodone or hydrocodone.

Most recently, Vladimir Putin decided to send Russian troops and weapons into an old-style battle for Ukraine, leading to the flight of about 10 million Ukrainian women and children, the embattlement of the Ukrainian men who were drafted to fight, the catastrophic destruction of many once-thriving Ukrainian cities and productive fields, the starvation of peoples of Africa and Asia because Russia has stopped the transport of foodstuffs from Ukraine, and a threat to every economy in the world, including the Russian economy.

All of this is happening against a backdrop of the most basic existential threat of our times - global climate change. A dramatic increase in the frequency and intensity of heat waves, drought, wildfires, floods, hurricanes, and tornadoes call for a revolutionary approach to ending the global reliance on fossil fuels and unprecedented behavioral changes in energy consumption.

The days, months, and years surrounding the Trump presidency, the birth of social media like Q-Anon, TikTok and Telegram, and the SARS-COV2 pandemic have all exacerbated a centuries-old risk of familial estrangement. In the U.S. during these years, widely diverging strains of revolutionary fervor have openly collided, resulting in a simmering undercurrent of civil war. One way to keep the simmer from reaching boiling point is for families – biological and otherwise – to ensure that we keep channels of respectful conversation open.

During these years, our family has grown in many ways while my husband and I eased into retirement. At the end of 2016, we celebrated the wedding of our daughter with family and friends, and the happy couple returned to Brooklyn to live. Six weeks later, our son met his life partner. For many reasons, they had a whirlwind courtship followed six months later by a wedding so secret, they didn't share the news with us until a few weeks after the fact. As of May 2022, our son and his wife have four children and work remotely, spending part of the year in each of three homes in three different states. In August 2020, our daughter and her husband moved from Brooklyn to North Carolina, also working remotely after the SARS-COV2 pandemic hit NYC. They bought a home and had their first child there in the fall of 2021.

Fully retired by early 2020, I had more time to devote to care of family members and the enjoyment of my new role as a grandmother. The delights of grandchildren have been a wonderful counterbalance to the disturbing news in the nation and world, inspiring me to challenge the darker aspects of the society surrounding us.

Our family's aging and personal growth made my husband and I realize it was time to adjust to new patterns of communication with our children, who had shifted into full adulthood. For older parents and their grown children, this adjustment involves a broad range of issues, from financial autonomy and different religious and political perspectives, to whether and when to share your own past work experiences or suggest job leads to them. The topics may include mundane questions such as how to interact effectively (Email? Text? Audio telephone? Video conference?), whether to share cell phone plans and streaming video passwords, or how to find the right balance of transparency and privacy about medical, dental, and emotional health.

This adjustment can sometimes be further complicated by any comments made by older parents – however benign or well-meaning – about their grown children's partners in love. At no point does the risk of tension ratchet further upward than it does when adult children have children of their own. Based on my conversations with many other older parents, these strains are true for everyone, although their intensity varies greatly depending on many factors that are simply out of your control. Positive adjustment to such major changes in life's roles often involves a fundamental personal revolution. You need to face the possibility that the aging of your parental role may reopen your own old wounds that your children never knew you had, and perhaps aggravate wounds that you never knew your children had. Finding ways to navigate these risks and tensions is crucial to avoid serious family estrangement.

One old friend told me of another mother about my age who had grown alienated from her adult son after he got married and had children. The estrangement was so serious that, two years after the alienation began, the mother died from an illness, and her son had never re-established contact with her, not even at her bedside as she slipped away. This severe estrangement is a horrific tragedy. If you want to prevent it from happening to you and your grown children, you and your children must become active listeners who avoid imposing past habits on the adults who happen to be your children or your parents.

Personally, I needed to remember how I had approached my own parents when I became a fully grown adult. I would prepare myself for visits by pretending that my parents were elderly strangers in a foreign land, that I was a guest in their home, and that I must treat them with the respect and manners I would use in such a situation. I would imagine that my past as their little child or teenager was in a large suitcase that I left behind. I have come to use the same approach with my grown children, but with the roles reversed – that is, they are young adult strangers from a foreign land, and I may not always understand their language or cultural habits, but I must treat them with the respect and courtesy that I would show to a younger foreign visitor.

Obviously, this approach has its limits, and parents and their adult children should want and need a greater intimacy than the relationship between foreign acquaintances. But greater intimacy is impossible without establishing and maintaining a foundation of respectful concern and discourse. While no one should accept trends toward illegal activity, violence, or suicide in family members without intervention, too often the alienation within families is based on far more trivial differences or disagreements.

As our nation and the world face the sobering reality of climate change, the prevention of family estrangement has never been more essential. All generations alive at this moment in history are called upon to work together to face the unavoidable consequences of climate catastrophe that humanity has wrought upon itself. To ensure the future survival of the youngest among us and their future progeny, we must be able to talk to each other now.

We need political, business, and spiritual leaders who can make this common purpose a central priority at every level in every nation on earth if humanity is to survive.

We also need leaders within our families – leaders who can build bridges across water poisoned by our failure to listen to each other with concern and compassion. If we find the will for this one common purpose – the survival of our children, grandchildren, and their progeny in all their diversity – then the other divisions between us have a chance to heal.

DECADE V PLUS: PIECES WRITTEN BETWEEN 2010 - 2022

In the Beginning Was the Word

November 2012

Watching crowds in New York City
The young man imagined a way
To get them to move and act in concert
To solve scientific puzzles
And develop models
For medical cures.

A game
The use of a game
And dialogue,
Constructive dialogue
For good.

We must apply his model
To politics
To climate change
To poverty.

Real science is what gives
Human life purpose
Understanding how something works
What it is

Books of revelations
Are efforts to understand
How the world works,
Re-examine the Bible
As a scientific and historical text
Written by people who were learning
To think and write, learning
How to figure things out.

If Rushdie is correct
And Muhammed was illiterate,
The Koran is not so different
From the Bible
Or Torah.
It's people
Writing about
Trying to figure things out.

In the beginning was the Word.
People who read the Torah, Bible, or Koran
Literally do not realize
That these Books
Are **stages** of human development
Not intended
To **stop** human development.

We are meant to keep exploring,
Keep testing, analyzing,
Keep trying
To figure things out.

2012

I am better off today than I was in November 2008.

I am no longer embarrassed to be an American citizen when I meet people from other parts of the world, as I was when George W. Bush was President.

My Individual Retirement Account is earning again, and this is crucial to me because I'm not getting any younger.

My youngest child has finished college, thanks partly to federal Parent Plus loans.

I was able to hire nine people over the past two years, thanks to the American Recovery and Reinvestment Act, and they contributed to development in my state. And because they succeeded at those temporary jobs, seven of those people have been able to get jobs subsequently.

I am proud to know that my gay friends can marry their lifetime partners in my state today, and that they can serve in the military without hiding their God-given sexual preference.

I feel more confident today than I did four years ago that my children will be able to obtain and afford health insurance as they fully enter the adult world, as long as the Affordable Care Act is not eviscerated by the Republicans.

With the memory of 9/11 crystal clear in my mind's eye, I feel safer today knowing that Osama bin Laden and many of his fellow Al Qaeda leaders are dead.

I am better off in so many ways, and I am grateful to President Barack Obama for his contribution to my well-being.

I am not disappointed in President Obama. I am disappointed by Supreme Court Justices Samuel Alito, Antonin Scalia, and Clarence Thomas. I am disappointed by John Boehner, Eric Cantor, and the rest of the House Republicans.

I am disappointed – no, I am saddened by – those of my fellow Americans who have allowed themselves to be fooled, against their own best interests, by the propaganda and fear-mongering of politicians like Paul Ryan, Newt Gingrich, and Reince Preibus; to be bought by the money of the Koch Brothers, Sheldon Adelson, the Perrys of Houston, and other billionaires who fight fair taxation and give lip service only to job creation in the U.S.; to be deceived by the distortions and incited by the hateful rhetoric of Fox News and Rush Limbaugh.

And yet, I am better off today than I was four years ago because, despite all these horrendous political shenanigans, I still believe in what Clark Kent symbolized – that truth, justice, and the American way — that democracy of the many good people – not plutocracy of the privileged few – will prevail.

Ruminations: November 2012

Nov. 6, 2012

It is the season for gratitude. I'm grateful to have a wonderful son who gave me a journal and encourages me to keep writing. I'm grateful that it is a clear sunny day after Hurricane Sandy and I can easily vote. I'm grateful that Barack Obama is on the ballot.

Nov. 11, 2012

Obama won! Again, I'm grateful for that, and that I saw the movie, "Inconvenient Truth" in 2006 and moved upstate and inland. But I'm brokenhearted to see the results of the Sandy storm on the people of Long Island, New York City, New Jersey and beyond.

Nov. 15, 2012

On a flight to Albuquerque to visit my sister for the first time in more than four years. My previous plans to visit were disrupted by the deaths of my mother- and father-in-law and the frequent trips that my husband took to help his mom. Getting onto this flight were four older people in wheelchairs. One woman appeared to be the wife or maybe sister of the man in the wheelchair. His mouth moved automatically back and forth as he held the ticket on his wheelchair, looking down at it in puzzlement.

All around, I see the men and women caring for the broken spouses, siblings, parents. I imagine how it might be when Barry and I reach that tipping point. I watch a PBS documentary about assisted suicide for those who are too old and sick to carry on, where a nonprofit group, out of compassion for the terminally suffering, put a bag over the person's head, while a loved one sits by and waits for the combination of sedative and asphyxiation to end the breathing and heartbeat and brain waves.

So, what is the start and end of a human life? Jon Stuart was unable to answer the argument that science says "life" begins at conception. But the real question is, when does that fetus reach the point where it can exist on its own, apart from the heart and blood and brain signals of the woman whose body houses and nurtures it?

If you believe in the soul, how can you know then that fetus becomes a separate individual? In all the years since Roe v. Wade, we haven't really addressed the shades of gray. We have, both sides, kept this issue in the Black and white zone. But these are much more ambiguous and hazy lines, at both ends of a human life.

Twenty-four weeks was the accepted point for the doctors for a long time. But technology keeps pushing the point back in both directions. This is two weeks shy of six months. So, when a woman wants a baby and is at risk of losing it, they will try to keep it alive, at enormous expense. And it is amazing and exciting that such a tiny creature that could fit into one hand can make it through into full existence as a separate person. But when a woman does not want that baby, whatever the reason, and it cannot survive outside her womb, even with our nature-opposing, high-tech medicine, then it is not capable of being an individual soul, a distinct human being.

For years, I have viewed the decisions about abortion as the woman's moral equivalent of men's decisions about going to war. The difference is that abortion, when performed prior to that point of separate life, is the end of a potential human being, while war involves the killing of fully realized, individuated persons.

2013

To: The New Yorker

George Parker's "Comment: Southern Discomfort" in your January 21 issue, contains an important grain of fact, but alas, the whole truth is more complex. A study of Google searches on racially charged terms and racist jokes, completed by Harvard doctoral candidate Seth Stephens-Davidowitz, was described in a June 9, 2012 piece in *The New York Times* (http://campaign-stops.blogs.nytimes.com/2012/06/09/how-racist-are-we-ask-google/). One of the geographic regions where such search terms are most heavily used is upstate New York, in areas that are represented in Congress by conservative Republicans.

Decades of disinvestment in these communities, once home to steel, auto, and related industries or to vibrant agricultural economies, has resulted in an increase in intolerance there. As Parker says of the "South's vices," violence, intolerance, aversion, and suspicion toward new ideas grow acute when communities are "marginalized and left behind." Some of the most entrenched poverty, lack of education and lost opportunity exists in rust belt and rural areas of the Northeast and Midwest. Our nation's abandonment of the people in these communities must be reversed if we are to work together, as President Obama asks us to do, toward a brighter future for all Americans.

To Joanna

Jan. 6, 2013

New Year
New start
Look back only for lessons learned
Look forward to a rising sun
Whether skies are cloudy or clear
The heavens in starry splendor
Even when cloaked
Offer constancy and comfort.

Long ago
My well-meaning mother
Choked a piece
Of her daughter's spirit
My lesson learned
To let you soar
And find your own
Gender-free trajectory.

What have you learned?
How will you use it tomorrow?
For life, love, joy
Making your way
Taking the risks
Feeling the pulse
As you ride the inevitable currents
Of sanguine flight.

Found Dead

Written Feb. 2014, after publishing *Unearthing the Ghosts* memoir. Unpublished.

On May 15, 1963, the body of my Aunt Leona Port was found somewhere near Willard State Hospital, the now-closed mental institution in the Finger Lakes where she had lived for decades. My siblings and I are Leona's only living relatives, and, because we are not direct descendants, we had to wait at least 50 years, under state law, to obtain her death certificate. I finally received a copy from the state's archives in January 2014.

The certificate says she "left hospital without consent," not that the institution was negligent in allowing Leona to wander away. "Found dead," the death record continues, "Schizophrenic. Catatonic type." The certificate is signed not by an independent examiner, but by a physician at the hospital who had "last seen the deceased alive on 5-11, 1963."

Leona's death certificate provided me with information for further research. In the case of a person who was "found dead," a newspaper story might have originated from police reports culled by a local paper's city desk. Using dozens of search terms to hunt through archives that store twentieth-century editions of newspapers from central New York, I've found no record of Leona's obituary nor any news item about the discovery of her body.

However, I did find news items from 1963 and 1964 reporting that three other "former patients at Willard State Hospital" had been "found dead" within 10 months of my Aunt Leona's death. William Fleming, age 73, had been missing from the hospital since May 20, 1963, five days after Leona's body was found. A construction worker discovered Fleming's body in an "abandoned barracks," according to the July 4, 1963 edition of the *Syracuse Post Standard*. Just 21 days later, in that paper's July 25th issue, the headline, "Body Recovered from Seneca Lake," refers to Glenn Campbell, age 64, another Willard patient reported missing on July 23, 1963. Both deaths were investigated, according to the paper, by the State Police.

Just eight months later, the *Post Standard* reported, "Willard Patient Found in Lake," when the body of Miss Evelyn Gould, age 66, was discovered in Seneca Lake. A former resident of New York City, Evelyn had been hospitalized at Willard since the previous August. The March 23, 1964 news item states, "It is believed she became confused and walked in the lake, police reported."

Could all four of these unattended deaths of state ward mental patients be completely coincidental? If a private hospital had four paying patients "found dead" within 10 months near the facility's premises, it is likely that there would be front page headlines and a major investigation. But I found no evidence in news archives that a public investigation of the Willard State Hospital took place in 1963 or 1964.

Willard was closed in 1995, and now New York State is about to consolidate a large number of other in-patient facilities for treating those considered mentally ill. Patient advocates are concerned whether the state will provide sufficient resources for community-based treatment centers as alternatives, and whether the remaining facilities will be adequate to meet the needs of the seriously ill.

Only 50 years ago, our state felt so little shame about four tortured souls who were "found dead" within 10 months that little or nothing was done publicly to determine the source of the problem at a state mental hospital. During our current transitions in mental health care, will we pay close enough attention and devote sufficient resources to people whom we label as "insane," "psychotic," or "mentally ill"?

August 9, 2014

Barry and I are on the public beach in Lake George, sipping gin and tonic, reading, relaxing on this fortieth anniversary of Richard Nixon's resignation. Fifty years ago, my family moved to Rome, New York. Now, on what used to be Griffiss Air Force Base, there is an industrial park where drones are being tested. The USA just used Navy jets to drop bombs on ISIS weapons in northern Iraq. The Israelis just resumed bombing Hamas-controlled Gaza after Hamas broke the cease-fire with 57 rockets. The Russians are returning the favor of sanctions for military action in Ukraine by placing an embargo on US and EU agricultural imports, and an Ebola epidemic is raging in West Africa.

I am using behavioral therapy and relaxation techniques and conscious breath awareness as tools to get to sleep and remain asleep in this frightening global turmoil, while praying to the spirits of loved ones who've passed away that Nathan's Harley rides will all be safe, and that Joanna lands the best teaching job for her in the fall. And, of course, Barry and I can stay gainfully employed until we're at least 66.

2015

Common sense and moral courage can prevail. We must ban sales of assault-type weapons and improve regulation on existing ownership. We need to stop sales of high-capacity gun magazines. Australia was successful with its buy-back program — we can do even better than that in the U.S. The Second Amendment only guarantees a right to a "well-regulated militia" but we now have anarchy in gun ownership and use.

We've seen enough violence. It's time to take action to reverse this deadly trend. One hundred percent background checks for gun sales is another good tool, and incentives to convert gun making factories to more constructive product manufacturing would help too. And for many, many reasons beyond gun violence, we must provide a stronger safety net for those who need mental health services in our nation. Our current system is a national disgrace. We must take better care of our people!

Crossing Over Borders

This has been a new season of death
Enough distance to know
It is not on my doorstep
Enough nearness to hear its call.

I see the exhaustion of wife and daughter
Tending to
Fading father and spouse.

Opening the condolence cards that,
Like all their lives together,
Were all about him,
Her sacrifice unseen
Unrewarded except by comfort
And successfully grown children.

Denial of loss
It is so tiring to wonder
If you are really sad
Or truly relieved.

To be oneself
Without another
To feel the freedom
Of loneliness.

And then there were the parents
Of a lost young woman
The mother's face twitching
As she strains to make small talk.
The father, once witty,
Simply staring into space
Posting entries
On his dead daughter's Facebook page
As if to say
She lives on
In social media space.

And Being Mortal
Is not just the title of a book.

I feel alive
But I am like all the rest
Just dying at my own pace,
Slow, deliberate
Clinging to late nights
To have more time.

How will I,
Will I
Be remembered?

Will anyone be there
To recall
And what stories will be told?

Facing life is just as hard
As facing death.

To my 16-year-old self

Jan. 3, 2016

A: Arbitration – you must learn to negotiate with both yourself and others.

B: Barry will be the true love of your life.

C: Care for yourself or no one else will.

D: Decisions are necessary and can be very hard.

E: Eleanor loves you, even when it seems that she doesn't.

F: Fred is an overgrown farm child who lost his mom at age seven – forgive him.

G: Grace is a part of your motion more than you see yourself.

H: Help is what you can receive and give.

I: Irate behavior does not become you and you must learn to control it.

J: Joanna is a child and young woman who will light up your life.

K: Keep your love of music close to your heart.

L: Living is a gift.

M: Marriage will turn out to be a great choice for you despite all the divorce around you.

N: Nathan will be like his name's sake to you – a gift of God that you will love to share with your family and friends.

O: Opera will surprise you.

P: Piano is something to which to return.

Q: Quixotic is a term that will sometimes define you.

R: "Reality is bad enough – you don't need to think about it too," is good advice from an ER doctor.

S: Security is not always necessary.

T: Time is something you must face.

U: Undervaluing your own achievements is contrary to your best interest, so don't do that!

V: Value family, friends, meaningful work, and play.

W: Wagner is a name you will want to keep for reasons that help to define you as a woman.

X: X-rays will show lots of arthritis as you age.

Y: Yes is the best answer in most situations.

Z: *Zealot* will be a book that will help you understand religion and politics much better than a Catholic catechism ever could.

Hiking Haiku Meta-Physics

July 26, 2016

Large clouds lead small puffs
South above Green Mountain tops
Slowly disappear

*

Electrons are lost
Until X and Y shake hands
And particles jump!

*

Green field before me
From there to me, unseen, sits
Field of gravity

*

Around and around
Specks of matter swirl with stars
Tucked away, earth spins

*

The things we don't see
Pulsate on, off, endlessly
Making up our world

2016:
The Simplicity of Medicare for All

In the October 15th Democratic candidate debate, Bernie Sanders and Elizabeth Warren were missing the point. In fact, they are missing several basic points they could deliver about the value of Medicare for All.

Insurance is all about risks. If all the people - whatever their health status, age, or gender - are in the same risk pool, with consistent coverage benefits pre-defined by law, the cost of those risks are spread across the entire population. That lowers the total cost of health care risks for everyone. And whether you admit it to yourself or not, everyone has health care risks, and you never know when and how they will hit you or how much they will truly cost.

But more important, Medicare for All produces the ultimate power when negotiating costs with hospitals, doctors, pharmaceutical companies, and even long-term care services. Huge corporations with hundreds of thousands of employees can provide better health insurance because the large size of their risk pool makes it feasible to spread risks and garner bargaining power to lower costs. Imagine the bargaining power when the coverage plan is consistent for all 372 million people in the United States. Medicare already sees this bargaining power. As AARP states, "Currently, 44 million beneficiaries—some 15 percent of the U.S. population—are enrolled in the Medicare program. Enrollment is expected to rise to 79 million by 2030."

Our current system, with its complex patchwork of hundreds of public and private health insurance plans, obscures the totality of health care costs. Worse, it dramatically drives the administrative costs for every facet of the health care delivery system. One of the best arguments in favor of Medicare for All is its simplicity.

Medicare for All could offer one consistent set of comprehensive benefits for every person in the United States. By offering comprehensive coverage, it can be far better than the current Medicare program, which requires seniors to seek supplemental coverage for health care costs that Medicare won't cover, such as dental care, long-term care, hearing aids, and other needed services.

Like most seniors, I currently pay premiums to the federal government for Medicare. I also pay premiums to the City of New York for the retiree group health insurance plan that my husband's former employer provided when he retired. In addition, I pay out of pocket for a portion of all of my medical bills.

I now make these premium and out of pocket payments to multiple sources, with the occasional surprises for high-cost prescription drugs, medical devices, or services that are not fully covered. I would prefer to have one predictable monthly bill that would cover my health care needs, whatever they are, especially if that one monthly bill is no higher, or even lower, than the total costs I'm now paying.

For me, that bill could be simply deducted from my Social Security check, just as my Medicare premium is now. Or it might be a combination of a Social Security check deduction and a tax bill. I don't really care who or how I pay that bill, as long as it is not going to lower my income. If I was still employed, that bill would be deducted from my paycheck, just as my premium share of my employer's health insurance was deducted from my paycheck when I was still an employee.

If I was self-employed, the bill would be part of the quarterly tax payment that I need to make. And I would be happy to have affordable access to health care, which is so hard to come by today if you're self-employed.

Simplicity. Bargaining power. Cost predictability. This is what the American people need. This is how our hospitals, medical providers, and pharmaceutical companies should be held accountable for costs. This is what Medicare for All can deliver. And this is how we can ensure that everyone has the basic human right to health care.

Dec. 25, 2016

Merry Christmas!

Joanna sounded very happy and excited on our call with her and Jack, and Nathan sounds good despite his split up with his Raleigh friend. He's settling into his new apartment, reconnecting with friends, and setting up a new drum kit.

In just a week, our dear daughter will get hitched! So happy that she met a good, kind man who loves and cares for her, and she has a second family of wonderful, supportive people.

I pray today that Nathan will also find the right life partner and get the peace of mind he deserves.

Barry will start a new job in February with the Bronx D.A., and we hope to find an apartment/second home in Yonkers – Getty Square near the train station. The entire situation has stressed out both of us, but at least the job situation is resolved in a positive way. The personal issue, we'll face together.

This is, of course, complicated by the sorry state of national affairs, after the election of Donald Trump.

Feb. 28, 2017

At a work conference, my mind drifts to the larger reality of the nation's capital in 2017. Everyone was questioning everything. A pundit writing an opinion piece explained why he called it "the age of disbelief." Heads were bowed toward electronic devices that had to be turned off into airplane mode when the planes took off. But even the respite of air travel evaporated as airline after airline provided free wi-fi on board, shortly after the planes were airborne.

Retired generals were calling for an investigation of Russian influence on the election held three months earlier. The newly inaugurated President blamed his enemies, who included, he said, the news media, for anything that might potentially cast him in a bad light. One by one, those who had voted against his female opponent and thus, for him, began to question what they had done in that voting booth in November. But now, it was too late. The hard-core supporters, the vile haters, had begun to run rampant. Signs of anti-Semitism overshadowed the Black Lives Matter movement, and the "pussy-grabbing" climate of misogyny began to flourish.

The haters always need a new object for their hate when the spotlight shifts. The President's son-in-law was one of their new targets. In the meantime, the White House team could see they were in way over their heads, with a boss who lacked any semblance of self-control in the early morning hours. Their opponents had grown increasingly frantic, bitter, and hostile. Those opponents were not tree huggers, singing Kumbaya. Using every political, legal, social media, satirical, and guerrilla tactic at their disposal, their opponents were engaging in full frontal intellectual combat.

The Second Amendment was up against the First Amendment. The question was really when the First Amendment advocates would use the Second to put a dictator out of office.

Aug. 31, 2017

Headed for semi-retirement.

This is the first time I will be replaced by someone who is my daughter's age. And my daughter is less than half the age I'll turn in one month, which is 65.

Setting out on a new course at earlier stages of my career was exciting, inspiring, and terrifying. While I feel a sense of unease this time, and some degree of fear, I have a strong sense of calm.

I see myself as a sailboat tacking toward the sunset on a breezy summer evening. I hear the clink of wine glasses held by old friends, toasting to my future success, which is to live a long, healthy life surrounded by people who love and care for you.

Nevertheless, I am sleepless tonight. I have a sense of anticipation, but also, as the Beatles song states, "that magic feeling, no place to go."

Drifting along with the gentle winds may be fine for tonight. But I know I must map a new course on this vast ocean. When I face aft, I see the wake I leave behind and all the waters I've traversed. But I know these seas can grow threatening in moments if the wind picks up or lighting flashes. Nature and the fates store surprises both pleasant and horrifying, especially in the last quarter of our lives.

So, I will look out over the bow, make my list of action items, check the point of sail, test the wind, and tack again. I will wish that young person well at her new job and make my own way towards a new horizon with a calm, steady hand at the helm. My keel is strong, and I've learned the hard way when to tack or jibe.

Still Seeking Justice Worth Restoring

Written in 2021 in the light of Black Lives Matter

Linda Mary Wagner

In 2021, Evanston, Illinois is being celebrated by many as the first locality in the USA to offer reparations to African Americans who faced housing discrimination there between 1919 and 1969. Unfortunately, housing is not the only form of discrimination.

While working as a freelance reporter in the greater Chicago area in 1986, I met an Evanston grandfather who stayed awake all night by the front window of the home he owned, his shotgun nearby. "They threw a Molotov cocktail through my window," the elderly Black man said. "My kids and grandkids live here. I worked hard for years to build this neighborhood. And now the police won't come when I call. So I have to protect my family myself."

African American gang members had infiltrated this quiet Black neighborhood with their crack deals. They retaliated after the grandfather called the police to stop them. For decades before, elders like him had provided essential services to affluent whites in other Evanston neighborhoods. But when this law-abiding Black man needed protection for his home and family, the police stopped responding.

A home invasion in this small city just north of Chicago had prompted me to report on an increase in crime there, leading me to meet the grandfather. That invasion was of my own home, the first that I and my husband owned in a predominantly white working-class neighborhood in Evanston called "milkman's row."

It was on an oppressively hot August night in 1986. My husband and I slept naked when we heard our six-month-old firstborn crying. I got up and warmed a bottle, not realizing that someone lurked outside the open kitchen window. After the baby calmed down, I went back to bed.

Soon our little one was crying again. "Your turn," I said, elbowing my husband. Moments later, my husband was yelling in the hallway. Fearing that the baby's head was caught in the crib bars, I flew out of bed and saw a masked man standing in the hall. I froze and screamed like a siren, while my husband ran into the nursery to get the baby. The stranger held his hand to his lips and shushed me as he backed away into the kitchen. The image of his physique, his red shirt, even of his neck between his mask and collar, and his wrists above his gloves, was seared into my mind.

My husband grabbed my arm and yelled, "Out the front door!" Buck naked, we ran into the street hollering, "Help! Police!" Neighbors rushed outside with blankets to cover us. In minutes, police cars arrived. They checked that no one remained in the house and saw that the screen in the kitchen window had been sliced open. They asked us to come inside, get dressed, and complete the report. The officers told us they were seeing an increase in home invasions, including some in which a woman alone was raped. In those cases, the police said, the descriptions matched that of this perpetrator in size, mask, physique, and the color of the skin on his wrist and neck.

We looked around. "My purse was on the kitchen table, and it's gone," I said. As we finished up, the police received an urgent call from another squad car a few miles away. "They're detaining somebody," the officer said. A woman in a nearby neighborhood had peered out her upper-floor window after hearing a dumpster clang and saw a man standing next to it. She watched as he dumped the contents of a purse into the garbage and peeled off an outer layer of clothes, including a red shirt.

"We need you to come with us to identify items from the purse that we recovered," the officer said to me. My husband remained home with the baby while the police drove me to a site where another police car was parked. They brought a tray to me with several items, including a set of keys. "Those are my keys, and those other things are from my purse," I said.

"The keys were on the man in that police car over there," an officer told me. "The other things were in the dumpster. We want to get him out of the car so you can identify him," said the cop. "He was masked," I said, haltingly, my voice and body shaking. "I remember his physique, but I didn't see his face. And I'm afraid to let him see me."

"We'll stand in front of you," said the officer. "Just tell us what you think when you see him." It had been only minutes since the masked man was standing in front of me in our home, so my impression was fresh and clear. Two officers emerged from the other car and pulled a young, handcuffed Black man out of the back seat. He was cursing and struggling until they made him stand still.

"Was this the man who was in your house?" an officer asked. I mentally measured the man in front of me now against the image etched in my memory. He stood about the same distance away from me as the masked man had been inside our house.

"His size and physique look the same as that man," I said.

"Are you sure?" he asked. "Yes," I said.

The first cops drove me home. The others brought the young man in front of our house and asked my husband to identify him. My husband gave the police the same caveats, saying his physique matched his very recent memory of the man who had broken into our home.

The case was handed over to the Cook County Attorney for prosecution. My husband was an attorney working then at a civil litigation firm. He and I were called to testify separately against the defendant, who was just 17 years old. His case was assigned to a young public defender.

What I still recall most clearly is the sound of my screams and the vision of a fit, trim young male stranger in my home urging me to silence my voice while I stood, without my consent, naked in front of him. On the witness stand, I was asked if I could identify, within the courtroom, the man who had entered our home illegally. I knew that the defendant in the courtroom was the same person whom police asked me to identify right after the crime.

"If he will stand up, I can identify him," I said. Without hesitation, the defendant stood up. His public defender made no objection and did not stop him from standing.

"That's him," I said.

Ultimately, the defendant entered a guilty plea and was sentenced to a five-year term in an Illinois state prison. In the course of my reporting, police told me that the defendant's father was in state prison, implying guilt by association. An officer also said they suspected him of murdering a sixteen-year-old on the day that he was released on bail from his arrest in our case. They showed me a drawing signed by the defendant that they found when searching his apartment. In it, a young man stands with a smoking gun over a bloody body.

One week after the break-in, I wrote this:

A masked spirit crept into our home space, as if he owned it himself. The next day, he's worse off. Another red-handed arrest with a good chance of some time to serve. The next day, I'm worse off too – terrorized, angry, suspicious of every sound that clings to my ears. He threatens the security of the two people most dear to me in this life – husband and child. He forces me to feel his injustices, life's injustice. He will not permit me to feel secure. His African ancestors or their white European colonizers sold his ancestors into slavery. His daddy is serving time in an Illinois prison. In a way, he remains enslaved, unschooled in and deprived of opportunities for change. He stays trapped because that's the only life he's permitted to know.

I want to have him sentenced to school, a job, the responsibility of children. I want him to write well enough to write me letter explaining why he did what he did and apologizing for the harm and trouble he caused. I want him sentenced to a job that will pay him enough to pay me back for what he stole from me. I want him sentenced to a moral education that will instill in him the understanding of his effect on other people and deep remorse for his mistakes.

I want JUSTICE. For me AND for him.

I didn't know then that there was a name for what I wanted – restorative justice. In 2020, the Marshall Project and *The Atlantic* published a joint

Investigation into restorative justice in murder cases, bringing victims' families in direct contact with the convicted murderer of their loved ones. The article defines restorative justice:

> *"...most victims say that what they most want from the criminal-justice system is safety for themselves and their communities. While some may seek vengeance, those who take part in restorative justice tend to believe that harsh punishment alone only creates further destruction and doesn't allow something productive to come from their loss."*

The article concludes that restorative justice can be healing, but it may not always work in murder cases. In my case, I'm not sure how my peace of mind could have been restored, but I sure would have preferred some type of alternative sentencing for the teenager who invaded my home, rather than the prison term he received.

It's been 34 years since that teenager broke into my home. Today, I'm 68 and I know I've benefited from white privilege my entire life. Given the recent attention to mass incarceration and policing of Black men, as well as the fear of crime that Donald Trump stirred during his presidency and campaigns, I've questioned over and over whether justice was served for me or for that young man. I have asked myself whether the officers tried to influence my testimony and reporting by speculating to me about other crimes the invader may have committed. I have wondered whether the police would have responded at all if my home had been in a Black neighborhood.

While cleaning out old files recently, I found records of our home invasion case. I had hoped that, after getting caught and paying his dues, our home invader turned his life around. But I've learned through online research of public records that he is now 52 years old, and incarceration did not rehabilitate him. After serving his first sentence, he was caught in another home invasion and other property crimes and sentenced to an additional 25 years. If, at the age of 17, he had received a sentence aimed at restorative justice and truly rehabilitative treatment, perhaps his future would have been brighter.

Perhaps others would have been spared from his later crimes. At this point, there is no way to know.

Surely crime victims, whatever our skin color, creed, or gender, do not want anyone else to become a victim of the crime we experienced. I suspect that most of us, including the Black grandpa and me, really want to see remorse in those who harm us and find ways of healing ourselves and our victimizers when that is possible.

We want crime prevented, and a sentence to our current prison system rarely accomplishes that. It is long past time to put into place programs and resources that have been proven to keep young men and women from trapping themselves - and all of us - in a destructive cycle of crime, punishment, and a counterproductive cycle of incarceration.

Linda's family, on vacation together in 2014.

Linda and Barry at a 2018 rally for democracy outside the Albany, NY Capitol building.

ON LOVE

My husband and I celebrated 50 years of togetherness in February 2023, around the time of Brazil's Carnaval and New Orleans' Mardi Gras. We became an "item" after dancing the evening away at a Carnaval celebration in chilly, snowy Buffalo, New York, hosted by Brazilian students at the University there. We were 21 years old, months before our birthdays in 1973. It was another six and a half years before we married in November 1979, and six and a half more years before our first child was born in February 1986.

As with any couple together so long, we have had our ups and downs. Each of us has habits that may annoy the other from time to time. But we have an enduring love that I believe will last 'til death do we part, and perhaps beyond.

Undated Eternal:
For Barry

The gift of humor lines your face
Softens your touch.
When you're gone
I miss our therapeutic
Giggling, bedtime faces,
Dinner deluge of talk.

I picture you
With hands in grease or dirt
Gripped around a wrench or saw,
Your hair uncombed,
Tossed like salad,
Eyes focused keenly,
A hopeful forehead crinkled
Yet not too sure.

You've seen me too,
Ill and weak,
Anxiety attacks,
Bad back, laid up.
In unspoken pathos you shared
Your strength, buttressed
My resistance
With your own will.

This is a simple barter
Between us,
My love for yours.
We don't consume each other
In our nova bursts of passion
But add orbits to our universe,
And reaching out beyond us,
Love begets love
A hundred times more.

ON CHILDREN

*Th*roughout our years together, before and after marriage, my (eventual) husband and I took turns wanting children and considering what impact children would likely have on our lives and our relationship with each other. Sometimes we hesitated because of our concerns about cruelties in the larger world. At other times, we worried about the divorce rate, our ability to provide financial support for a growing family, or our careers.

By 1984, after 11 years as a couple and five years as wife and husband, we agreed to take the plunge. Prior to a woman's access to birth control, pregnancy was rarely a choice. It happened whether you intended it or not. But when a woman's reproductive rights are guaranteed, having children or not is a question and a decision. The choice to have children, or at least to try, involves the acceptance that we do not have control over all aspects of our lives.

For me and Barry, the decision to have children was one of the sweetest, most rewarding decisions of our lives. Our first was a son, born in February 1986; our second was a daughter, born in August 1989.

Children create a personal revolution in your life, with everything from the mundane schedules of sleeping, eating, and recreation to the most profound joys and responsibilities.

Linda with her daughter's and son-in-law's baby boy in 2021.

At Duke Gardens in North Caroline, November 2021,
Linda with her children and grandchildren.

Linda with her son and daughter-in-law's baby boy in 2022.

Linda with her children and grandchildren in November
2022 on the beach in North Carolina.

EPILOGUE

August 25, 2022

In mid-May 2022, our son called to say that his fourth child – and our fifth grandchild – was born healthy and strong. Since his wife had been very sick early in the first trimester when she didn't yet realize that she was pregnant, we were relieved and excited to hear the good news. In early September 2021, our daughter texted that her newborn was healthy and thriving. This also came with a sigh of relief; she had experienced a tough early labor and delivery after developing pre-eclampsia. We saw our daughter gradually recover from the many impacts on her own health. Coinciding with Rosh Hashanah, ushering in the year 5782, her good news was especially sweet.

And yet, this sweetness is tempered by other, broader concerns about the outlook for the health of these babies, their parents, and all our world's children and grandchildren. Late last year, I read that the world's leading medical journals issued an unprecedented joint statement, warning that climate change is the "greatest threat" to global public health and urging the world's leaders to cut heat-trapping emissions to avoid "catastrophic harm to health that will be impossible to reverse."

While the world has focused since early 2020 on the SARS-COV2 global pandemic and the resulting high tides of illness and death from the resulting COVID 19 illness and deaths, the climate change that underlies emerging illnesses like this has also wreaked havoc with out-of-control wildfires, droughts, floods, and destruction to all living things.

To keep a world intact for our children, grandchildren, and their future offspring, I am called to a new global revolution. It is not that different than the call I heard more than five decades ago, on the first Earth Day in 1970. To enable humanity to survive, I must now devote myself to ending the human contribution to climate change.

This revolution requires radical change, including an end to senseless wars that destroy eco-systems around the world. It demands the reproductive freedom of women, to manage the explosion of the global human population. It needs rigorous controls on our own behaviors – on my and your own behaviors – to dramatically reduce the carbon emissions that are choking life on earth. It demands a turnaround of the mass suicidal activities that have plagued humankind since I was born.

This revolution requires national and business leaders to make a total commitment to ending our reliance on fossil fuels and the greenhouse gases that are choking our planet. We must demand this commitment from our leaders.

I hope you will join me in this revolution. For you and your family, for me and my family, for each one of us in the human family. The time for this revolution is now.

2018 Rally for democracy outside the Capitol building in Albany, New York.

APPENDICES

Green Grandma for Climate Action

When I completed this manuscript, I realized it was not enough to call for climate action unless I offered some guidance to my readers about how to take such action. To provide you with climate action resources, solutions, and news, I have created a "Green Grandma" website. You can find it at:

https://LindaMaryWagner.com

OR https://GreenGrandmas.org

At the time of publication, there is no Green Grandmas organization in the U.S. But I hope my book and website can help to create one!

Follow-up to "Still Seeking Justice Worth Restoring."

To find constructive guides to restorative justice, a good place to start is the nonprofit Marshall Project. You can find them online at www.themarshall-project.org.

1. https://www.themarshallproject.org/2017/01/17/dear-president-trump-here-s-how-to-get-right-on-crime-part-1

2. https://www.themarshallproject.org/2017/03/13/crime-hotspots-need-investments-not-just-policing

3. https://www.prisonpolicy.org/research/recidivism_and_reentry/

4. https://www.correctionsone.com/re-entry-and-recidivism/articles/6-evidence-based-practices-proven-to-lower-recidivism-MRzqFIO9P1okPNBF/

5. https://www.brennancenter.org/our-work/analysis-opinion/ community-organizations-have-important-role-lowering-crime-rates

6. https://www.apa.org/monitor/julaug03/youth

7. https://news.siu.edu/2019/01/012819-community-based-programs-may-help-reduce-crime-rates.php

8. https://www.mhanational.org/issues/ access-mental-health-care-and-incarceration

9. https://www.nami.org/Advocacy/Policy-Priorities/ Divert-from-Justice-Involvement/Jailing-People-with-Mental-Illness

10. https://www.psycom.net/how-to-reduce-mental-illness-in-prisons/

11. https://dualdiagnosis.org/drug-rehab-instead-of-prison-could-save-billions-says-report-2/

12. https://www.oxfordtreatment.com/rehab-vs.-prison/

ABOUT THE AUTHOR

Linda Mary Wagner is the author of the self-published book, *Unearthing the Ghosts: A Mystery Memoir*, a coming-of-age story of trauma and recovery set in upstate New York. She has four decades of leadership experience in local, state, and national nonprofit organizations, including Associated Press, Consumers Union/Consumer Reports, the NYS Association of County Health Officials, and the Institute for Music and Neurologic Function. Earlier in her career (1976-1990), she was a freelance journalist for NPR and numerous other print, radio, and TV news outlets. Ms. Wagner earned her MPA from Columbia University's School of International Public Affairs and her BA from the University at Buffalo. Married for more than 40 years to the same guy, she is the mother of an adult son and daughter and has five grandchildren who call her Nana. She lives with her husband in Albany, New York and considers herself a Green Grandma for Climate Action Now. *Rear-View Reflections on Radical Change: A Green Grandma's Memoir and Call for Climate Action* is her second book.